Verdict on the Crash:
Causes and Policy Implications

Verdict on the Crash: Causes and Policy Implications

EDITED BY PHILIP BOOTH

WITH CONTRIBUTIONS FROM

JAMES ALEXANDER

MICHAEL BEENSTOCK

PHILIP BOOTH

EAMONN BUTLER

TIM CONGDON

LAURENCE COPELAND

KEVIN DOWD

JOHN GREENWOOD

SAMUEL GREGG

JOHN KAY

DAVID LLEWELLYN

ALAN MORRISON

D. R. MYDDELTON

ANNA SCHWARTZ

GEOFFREY WOOD

The Institute of Economic Affairs

First published in Great Britain in 2009 by
The Institute of Economic Affairs
2 Lord North Street
Westminster
London SW1P 3LB
in association with Profile Books Ltd

The mission of the Institute of Economic Affairs is to improve public understanding of the fundamental institutions of a free society, by analysing and expounding the role of markets in solving economic and social problems.

A CIP catalogue record for this book is available from the British Library.

ISBN 978 0 255 36635 9

Many IEA publications are translated into languages other than English or are reprinted. Permission to translate or to reprint should be sought from the Director General at the address above.

Typeset in Stone by MacGuru Ltd
info@macguru.org.uk

Printed and bound in Great Britain by Hobbs the Printers

CONTENTS

PART TWO: THE REGULATORY RESPONSE

ABOUT THE AUTHORS

James Alexander

James Alexander holds a PhD in Economic History on late seventeenth-century London from the LSE. He was Research Editor at *The Banker* for three years, before working for various investment banks as a sell-side banks' analyst. He has been on the buy-side analysing banks at M&G Investment Management for seven years, as well as currently being Head of Equity Research.

Michael Beenstock

A graduate of the London School of Economics, Michael Beenstock was initially employed as an economist at HM Treasury and the World Bank. Subsequently he joined the London Business School and City University Business School. Since 1987 he has been Professor of Economics at the Hebrew University of Jerusalem.

Philip Booth

Philip Booth is Editorial and Programme Director of the Institute of Economic Affairs and Professor of Insurance and Risk Management at the Sir John Cass Business School, City University. He has written extensively on regulation, social insurance and Catholic social teaching. He is a fellow of the Institute of Actuaries and of the Royal Statistical Society and Associate Editor of *Annals of Actuarial Science* and the *British Actuarial Journal*. He has also advised the Bank of England on financial stability issues (1998–2002).

Eamonn Butler

Dr Eamonn Butler is Director of the Adam Smith Institute. He has written introductions to the economists F. A. Hayek, Milton Friedman, Ludwig von Mises and (for the IEA) Adam Smith. His recent books include *The Best Book on the Market* and *The Rotten State of Britain*.

Tim Congdon

Tim Congdon is an economist and businessman. He founded Lombard Street Research in 1989 and between 1992 and 1997 was a member of the Treasury Panel of Independent Forecasters (the so-called 'wise men'), which advised the Chancellor of the Exchequer on economic policy. His latest book, *Central Banking in a Free Society*, was published by the Institute of Economic Affairs in March 2009.

Laurence Copeland

Laurence Copeland is Professor of Finance at Cardiff Business School Investment Management Research Unit. He researches and publishes on stock and bond markets, derivatives and exchange rates. He has also been an occasional consultant to a number of major financial institutions and has held visiting posts at universities in Europe, the USA and Asia.

Kevin Dowd

Kevin Dowd is Professor of Financial Risk Management at the Nottingham University Business School. He has a PhD in economics and has written extensively on monetary economics and macroeconomics, financial regulation, free banking, financial risk management, pension economics and political economy. He has affiliations with the Cato Institute, the Institute of Economic Affairs, the Taxpayers' Alliance, the Pensions Institute, the Independent Institute and the Open Republic Institute.

John Greenwood

John Greenwood is chief economist at Invesco, a global fund management company. In 1983, as editor of *Asian Monetary Monitor*, he proposed a currency board scheme for stabilising the Hong Kong dollar that is still in operation today. An economic adviser to the Hong Kong Government (1992–3), he has been a member of the Currency Board Committee of the Hong Kong Monetary Authority since 1998. His book *Hong Kong's Link to the US Dollar: Origins and Evolution* was published in 2007.

Samuel Gregg

Dr Samuel Gregg is Director of Research at the Acton Institute. He has written and spoken extensively on questions of political economy, economic history, ethics in finance and natural law theory. His most recent book is the prize-winning *The Commercial Society* (2007).

John Kay

John Kay is a Fellow of St John's College, Oxford, a Visiting Professor of Economics at the London School of Economics and a director of several public and private companies. He was Professor of Economics at the London Business School and Professor of Management at the University of Oxford. He has been director of an independent think tank and set up and sold a highly successful economic consultancy business. He now writes a weekly column for the *Financial Times*. His latest book, *The Long and the Short of It – Finance and Investment for Normally Intelligent People Who Are Not in the Industry* – was published in January 2009.

David Llewellyn

David Llewellyn is Professor of Money and Banking at Loughborough University, Honorary Visiting Professor at the Sir John Cass Business

School in London, and Visiting Professor at the Swiss Finance Institute in Zurich and the Vienna University of Economics and Business Administration. He is Consultant Economist to ICAP plc. Previous career appointments include serving as an economist at Unilever (Rotterdam), HM Treasury (London) and the International Monetary Fund (Washington). Between 1994 and 2002 he was a Public Interest Director of the Personal Investment Authority. He serves as a consultant to financial firms, management consultancy firms and regulatory agencies in several countries.

Alan Morrison

Alan Morrison is Professor of Finance at the Saïd Business School of the University of Oxford, and a Fellow of Merton College. His research work is in the fields of corporate finance and the microeconomics of banking. Among the journals in which he has published are the *American Economic Review*, the *Journal of Finance*, the *Journal of Financial Economics* and the *Journal of Financial Intermediation*.

D. R. Myddelton

D. R. Myddelton is Emeritus Professor of Finance and Accounting at Cranfield University. He has written many textbooks on finance and accounting and other books on the British tax system, government project disasters, inflation accounting, accounting standards and margins of error in accounting. He is Chairman of the Institute of Economic Affairs.

Anna Schwartz

Anna Schwartz has worked at the US National Bureau of Economic Research since 1941. She co-authored, with Milton Friedman, *A Monetary History of the United States 1867–1960*, published in 1963. She has written widely on the relationship between monetary stability and financial stability and has also published academic work on inflation, interest rates, foreign exchange markets and monetary standards.

Geoffrey Wood

Geoffrey Wood is Professor of Economics at the Sir John Cass Business School, London, and Professor of Monetary Economics at the University of Buckingham. In the past he has worked in the Bank of England, where for many years he served as Special Adviser on Financial Stability, and in the US Federal Reserve System. He has acted as an adviser to the New Zealand Treasury, is a director of an investment trust, and a member of the investment advisory panel of a large pension fund. He has also been economic adviser to two stockbroking partnerships, and to a bank. He is Specialist Adviser to the Treasury Select Committee of the House of Commons. He has published fourteen books and over a hundred professional papers in the fields of banking, monetary policy and regulation. The present paper is written in a personal capacity.

FOREWORD

The typical view of the financial market crash of 2008 is that it resulted from the unrestrained misbehaviour of bankers arising from the absence of proper regulatory constraints. While bankers may not have behaved as prudently as we would have hoped, we need to ask 'why not?' Lack of regulation cannot be the main answer as there have clearly been times when financial markets have been regulated much more lightly. If we do not look for the underlying, as opposed to the popularly assumed, causes of the financial crash then we will conclude, as our prime minister has, that regulatory oversight must be tightened.

The first part of this book examines many possible causes of the collapse in banking and other financial markets. The government institutions that control monetary policy seem to have been at fault – both here and in the USA. Regulators have taken actions that have encouraged the very forms of behaviour that they now criticise. Additionally, the types of regulation that did exist were inappropriate, over-prescriptive and generally missed the big picture.

Even if the crisis had an element of poor market practice at its roots, the performance of government institutions should be raising doubts in people's minds as to whether agencies of the state are likely to be any more effective than market mechanisms in preventing another crisis.

In general, the authors in Part Two share this scepticism. They do argue, however, that the nature of banking is such that some regulation is required. That regulation ought to involve, suggest the authors, precisely targeted objectives and tools of intervention to ensure that regulators can be called properly to account and do not suffer from 'mission creep'. This would surely be better than the labyrinthine rule books that currently govern people's behaviour in financial markets.

I recommend this publication to all who are interested in the catastrophic events in financial markets over the last two years and who want to ensure that appropriate policy action is taken to reduce the likelihood of such events happening again.

The views expressed in this monograph are, as in all IEA publications, those of the authors and not those of the Institute (which has no corporate view), its managing trustees, Academic Advisory Council Members or senior staff.

JOHN BLUNDELL
Director General and Ralph Harris Fellow
Institute of Economic Affairs
March 2009

SUMMARY

- To some degree, UK and US monetary policy was to blame for recent problems in financial markets, thus replicating previous boom and bust episodes both in the UK and overseas.
- US government policy, by encouraging banks to lend to people with poor credit records, was a contributory factor in undermining US banks' balance sheets. This problem was exacerbated both by the presence of the securitisation agencies, Fannie Mae and Freddie Mac, and by dishonest behaviour by some US borrowers.
- International bank capital regulation did not reduce the risk of insolvency. It may have contributed to the crisis, however, by encouraging all banks to have similar risk models, by lulling banks' counterparties into a false sense of security and by making banks accountable to regulators rather than to market participants.
- Both international and domestic regulation also encouraged banks to make their activities more opaque than would otherwise have been the case, thus contributing to the build-up of risk.
- The management of the crisis by the UK public authorities exacerbated the problems rather than eased them. Both the slow reaction of the Bank of England and the use of market-value accounting rules in inappropriate circumstances made liquidity problems in the wholesale banking market worse.
- Market monitoring of banks was less effective than it should have been. The presence of regulation was probably a contributory factor to this. Banks over-leveraged, however, in ways that, *ex post*, were clearly inappropriate.
- Short selling by hedge funds played no significant part in the crisis.

The use by regulators of credit ratings to set regulatory capital has undermined their integrity. As such, attempts to regulate ratings agencies and hedge funds further are likely to be damaging.

- While regulators might now understand how to prevent the crash of 2008 from happening again, they have demonstrated that they have no special gifts of foresight that justify confidence in the view that regulation would be effective in preventing future problems in financial markets. In general, the public authorities welcomed the innovations in financial markets that many commentators suggest are at the root of the problems we face now.

- Public choice economics suggests that financial market regulation should be based on very clear principles, with regulators being given specific objectives. This involves a complete reversal of recent trends in financial regulation.

- The most important specific objective that should be given to bank regulators is the protection of the payments system. Regulation should also ensure that those who provide capital to a bank should not be sheltered from the risks.

- Specific legal mechanisms should be brought in to achieve these goals. A variety of approaches is possible, and these would not involve detailed regulation of the activities of banks.

- Such an approach to regulation would ensure that the risk of failure fell squarely on a bank's shareholders and counterparties rather than on taxpayers.

EDITOR'S PREFACE

In popular folklore, the causes of the crash of 2008 are pretty clear. Unregulated financial markets were allowed to run wild, creating new products that nobody understood; short-term profits were put ahead of the importance of ensuring a long-term return; and incentive structures were such that huge bonuses were paid to bankers while they destroyed the value of their companies, thus putting the whole economy at risk. This may or may not be true as a partial explanation, but folklore has also gone on to suggest that these problems demonstrate that what is needed is more intrusive systems of financial regulation. There has been no better manifestation of this than the comments by the Archbishop of Canterbury and the Archbishop of York, who made these very points, in one case in rather colourful language.

Events that produce serious consequences require serious analysis, however. Off-the-cuff remarks and shallow thinking could, in fact, lead us to take action that will make a recurrence of the crash more likely rather than less likely. Indeed, it is quite possible to so seriously misdiagnose the causes of the crash that diametrically wrong conclusions are reached as to the appropriate policy action. It is for this reason – effectively to avoid the mistakes made by President Roosevelt after the Great Depression and many Western governments in the following years – that it is to important to examine carefully what went wrong.

In the first part of this monograph, the authors look at the various causes of the financial crash of 2008. Each possible cause is considered briefly with, where appropriate, tentative ideas being put forward for policy action. The second part examines more specifically the appropriate regulatory response. Where a new approach to regulation is needed, the authors suggest well-defined regulatory intervention based on sound economic principles. In Part One, however, many of the authors, all eminent academics or financial market practitioners, conclude that earlier attempts to regulate financial markets have exacerbated the problems we have faced in the financial system. Regulation can have unforeseen consequences and thus it needs to be well targeted and with a specific objective.

Verdict on the Crash:
Causes and Policy Implications

PART ONE
THE CAUSES OF THE CRASH OF 2008

1 INTRODUCTION

Philip Booth

Part One of this monograph investigates various causes of the financial markets crash of 2008. Some of the chapters also look at what might be described as 'red herrings' – supposed causes of the crash that, in reality, were of trivial importance. This introductory chapter provides a summary of the ideas expressed by the authors and some commentary on their conclusions.

The causes of the crash

Monetary policy

In Chapters 2 and 3, John Greenwood and Anna Schwartz analyse the problems caused by inappropriate monetary policy. It is now widely accepted that the boom and bust, culminating in the Great Depression of the 1930s, arose as a result of catastrophically mismanaged monetary policy. The same is true of the Japanese boom, bust and malaise of the late twentieth century. So, it is natural that we should start by examining monetary policy to see whether that is the culprit again: and so it turns out to be. Loose monetary policy in the USA over an extended period of time, and in the UK over a shorter period of time, led to a financial bubble. Low interest rates led to monetary aggregates expanding, an asset-price boom, low saving and increased consumption and investment. These, in turn, led to a substantial misallocation of resources. Higher asset prices raised the value of collateral against secured loans and thus encouraged more lending and higher leverage while reducing the apparent risk faced by lenders and borrowers. Consumer price inflation remained subdued, to a degree, as the relative price of tradable goods fell. Loose monetary policy will always have an impact on the economic system, however, and the particular manifestation of loose monetary policy in the early 21st century was an asset-price and credit boom – with credit often being secured against higher asset values.

So, rather than looking at inherent instabilities in supposedly free financial markets as the first cause of the crash, we should probably look at the instabilities caused by government-controlled monetary policy. But, even if this were the first cause of the boom and crash it does not follow that there are no implications for financial market management and regulation. Even if we have better-designed institutions for the conduct of monetary policy, mistakes will still happen. We therefore need financial markets that are robust in the face of monetary policy mistakes. Will more robust financial markets be a product of more regulation? The authors of this book throw substantial doubt on that hypothesis.

Regulation

Eamonn Butler and, again, Anna Schwartz show how government regulation actually encouraged US institutions to lend to bad risks. The US government was also strongly supporting the process of securitisation of mortgages through its corporatist, nominally private, institutions Fannie Mae and Freddie Mac. Indeed, central banks, governments and regulators across the world seemed supportive of the process of securitisation that created many of the instruments that led to later trouble. Paul Tucker, recently promoted to Deputy Governor of the Bank of England, said in a speech as late as April 2007: 'So it would seem that there is a good deal to welcome in the greater dispersion of risk made possible by modern instruments, markets and institutions.'[1] There are two lessons from this. The first is that intervention by government in financial markets played a part in the events that led up to the crash

---

1   Seehttp://www.bankofengland.co.uk/publications/quarterlybulletin/qb070211.pdf. This remark was qualified later in the speech.

– in other words government failure should be the object of serious attention. The second is that, even if one does not accept that government action was a considerable contributory factor in the boom and following crash, it is quite clear that government agencies did not spot it coming before market participants did. We should not, then, assume that government agencies can 'correct' market failure. In other words, if the conditions that ensure that markets themselves avoid serious error are lacking, it should not be assumed that governments can create these conditions and make markets work better.

There is, indeed, the likelihood that financial market regulation made matters worse and not better. After Butler's chapter, this problem is discussed further in the chapters by Beenstock, Dowd and Alexander. It may be overstating the point to argue that the crash was caused by government failure but it certainly appears that there is nothing that governments and regulators have done that made the crash less likely or made its consequences less dire. International banking regulation encourages the creation of opaque financial instruments. The increased focus on regulation at an international and European Union level necessarily means that regulation either has to be more complex to deal with a greater variety of industry structures and practices or that it is unsuitable in the case of many countries. Because gearing and capital are regulated, banks find more and more opaque ways to obtain the effect of gearing without doing the things that regulators penalise. This leads to the creation of complex financial instruments and structures that few within, never mind outside, the industry understand. Risk taking is therefore harder for shareholders to monitor and penalise. Furthermore, regulators encouraged all financial institutions to use similar quantitative risk models for setting their capital and assessing risks. It is quite possible that these models were flawed. Certainly they seemed unable to assess extreme risks effectively (see, in particular, the chapter by Dowd).

This all led to several serious consequences. First, the process of trial and error in the conduct of risk measurement and modelling was blunted. If the models were to go wrong for one financial institution, then they were likely to go wrong for them all – at the same time. The models also encouraged financial institutions to take similar risks, which were assessed, generally, using historical data. This meant that institutions would react in similar ways when things went wrong and this would lead to consequences that would not be captured by the models. In particular, when institutions became distressed they all rushed for the exit, leading to fire sales and illiquidity. Conceptual thinking about risk was discouraged and complexity was encouraged by the regulatory emphasis on complex modelling. Those who should have been monitoring banks (such as shareholders) were reassured that risk was being kept in bounds, even though the extent of the risks they were taking could not be understood at a conceptual level: knowledge replaced understanding.

A diversion – the Austrian justification for the market economy

This trend, it should be added, was encouraged by modern ideas in economic theory, as well as by regulators. It is all reminiscent of the calculation debate of the 1920s and 1930s. The socialists, in that debate, were able to point to neoclassical economic theory with its quantitative and static approach and argue that a socialist central planning authority could reproduce the equilibrium of a market economy more efficiently. The Austrian response was that the economy is dynamic, responding to new information that is discovered by all participants in the market at any time. It is therefore meaningless to talk about market prices reflecting all information – the purpose of a market is to discover and reflect new information, a process that is continuous and that cannot be replicated by central planning. In modern finance, there has been a triumph, at the intellectual level, of the neoclassical approach. Financial markets are often assumed to be efficient (that is, they take into account all information at any time). Markets are assumed to follow regular patterns and the probability distribution of outcomes is assumed to be predictable using highly quantitative models. Sadly, the logic of the calculation debate has been played out exactly as the socialists hoped and the Austrians feared. These neoclassical justifications for a free market were absorbed into a socialist system of financial regulation which used market mechanisms and market information as its main pillars. Thus stewardship accounting, based on professional judgement and disclosure, was replaced by accounting based on market values; highly quantitative models based on past statistical patterns were certified by regulators to measure risk and determine capital requirements; market-based credit ratings were important in bank capital setting; and so on.

This was described by some as the 'triumph of the free market'. In fact, it was the triumph of the socialist belief that planners and regulators could use prevailing market prices as if they were static entities that reflected all information.

In the process, market participants are lulled into a false sense of security. There was little competition in approaches to risk management and capital setting (indeed, little competition was allowed). And those institutional mechanisms that can be used to control or reduce risk, which arise because people are aware of their ignorance (for example, keeping financial institutions simple), were crowded out or regarded as unnecessary. Furthermore, the uniform ways of measuring risk based on market information themselves affected behaviour in ways that made the models invalid.

How regulation disorientated relationships

Financial regulation also caused market participants to create a fundamentally disordered set of processes. Instead of releasing information to the market, financial institutions' most important relationships were often with the regulators. The least-regulated financial institutions, it appears, were those that bore least responsibility for and were least affected by the crash.

Also, just as some have argued that there were distorted incentives within banks caused, for example, by high bonuses and limited liability – an error that the market can correct – there are also distorted incentives structurally embedded within regulators. Regulators have an incentive to be too cautious because they do not want problems to arise on their watch for which they will be held responsible. Paradoxically, once a problem arises, regulators have an incentive to delay action so as not to draw attention to it. First, they may hope that an improvement in the markets will make the problem go away. Second, as Beenstock points out, many regulators seek jobs with institutions that they have regulated – they may well not wish to treat such institutions too harshly.

Regulatory failures during the crash

There were also central bank, regulatory and government failures during the course of the events of 2007 and 2008. With regard to the central bank's reaction to the events in financial markets, Tim Congdon finds that the Bank of England did not do what could have been reasonably expected and did not take the action that could have prevented the liquidity crisis that developed in financial markets. D. R. Myddelton deals specifically with the problems caused by mark-to-market accounting standards. As asset markets spiked, these accounting standards required companies to take assets into their accounts at full value, even if they would have preferred to use more prudent methods. As market values crashed, much-reduced values had to be taken into accounts, even if there was no viable market in the securities concerned. This promoted the downward spiral of lower assets values, capital calls, a rush to liquidity, asset sales, lower asset values and so on.

Market failures – red herrings and genuine problems

This all leads to the question of whether actors within financial markets were at all culpable. Was the crash simply a symptom of government failure, while participants in financial markets behaved like angels?

Of course, this is not the case. But, first, we should deal with a couple of red herrings. Some have put the blame on short sellers increasing market volatility and bringing down the banks. The Archbishop of York compared short sellers with robber barons. Laurence Copeland deals directly with this myth. There is no inherent difference between reducing a long position and going short in a security. Furthermore, there is simply no evidence that short-selling activity had anything to do with bringing down the banks. Indeed, if anything, short selling increased information flows in markets that were desperately short of information.

The second red herring is the supposed culpability of the credit rating agencies. Alan Morrison admits that they may well have made mistakes – for example, by coalescing on the same kind of modelling techniques, thus making alternative rating agencies' opinions insufficiently different. New financial regulations have often based regulatory capital requirements on credit ratings, however. A highly rated bond is a passport to lower capital requirements. Thus, both purchasers and issuers of asset-backed securities may care more about being able to get a good rating than getting an accurate rating. This weakens the incentives for rating agencies to ensure that their ratings are sound.

David Llewellyn and Samuel Gregg write more directly about the culpability of market participants. Llewellyn believes that banks have made big mistakes by departing from the traditional model of banking. They have, of course, lost huge amounts of money as a result (between 90 and 100 per cent of the equity value in some cases), as well as imposing wider economic losses on society at large. Once again, the problem with proposing regulatory responses to such so-called market failures is that they assume that the regulator can act more quickly and with greater foresight than market participants themselves. Llewellyn finds no evidence to suggest that this is likely to be the case: regulators were behind the curve and banks' owners will learn from their mistakes having made such large losses.

Gregg, as a philosopher rather than an economist, treats his subject in a different style from the other authors. He believes that trust and prudence have become scarce among both borrowers and lenders alike. Of course, trust and prudence are valuable attributes that should command a premium in the market (lower interest rates for borrowers and more custom for lenders). It is clear that borrowers lied on mortgage proposal forms. Again, this observation of what some would call market failure does not provide us with normative lessons for the role of regulation. It could be argued that compliance with regulation has displaced trust and that no amount of additional regulation in financial markets in the last twenty years has done anything to increase the level of trust. And perhaps a reliance on regulation has also crowded out the processes whereby institutions take responsibility for the risks that they underwrite and has discouraged them from undertaking due-diligence checks in their relationships with other market participants. Gregg argues that the values that should underpin markets are learned in the family and in places of education and cannot be created by regulation. Taking the chapter by Gregg, together with that by Butler, we learn the lesson that we should be careful about giving regulators and governments the power to regulate interest rates charged to and the volume of loans given to the poor. Whenever such matters become the subject of regulation, political considerations and not economic and social considerations predominate. Hence, as Butler shows, governments in practice have used their powers to promote borrowing among those least able to afford to borrow.

Conclusion

The authors in this first section do not suggest that there need to be no changes to the way in which financial markets are regulated. They do, however, lay to rest convincingly the idea that more regulatory intervention is the appropriate response to the crisis of 2008. To a large extent government institutions were responsible for what happened. In so many different ways central banks, central governments and regulators took decisions that, in turn, encouraged the private sector to take decisions that they might well have avoided had there been no intervention. Furthermore, it certainly was not the case that government institutions showed the foresight, discretion, wisdom and competence that would suggest that more regulatory intervention, rather than less, would have made the crash less dramatic or its consequences less grave. There has been market failure because markets are not perfect – markets involve a discovery process and respond to errors made by market participants. Government failure has been no less evident than market failure and regulation has often encouraged market participants to make errors. Indeed, the fact that regulation has often encouraged many market participants to make similar errors at the same time is particularly unfortunate.

Markets will learn from their mistakes and the market has punished banks that made mistakes. But will regulators learn from their mistakes and is the political system capable of providing incentives to regulators to ensure that they do? How we should respond in the field of regulatory policy is discussed in Part Two.

2 THE SUCCESSES AND FAILURES OF UK MONETARY POLICY, 2000–08

John Greenwood

Introduction

The period 2000–08 neatly divides into two sub-periods: the first five years from 2000 until the end of 2004, when monetary policy proved highly successful, and the three-year period from 2005 until the beginning of 2008 when monetary policy essentially went off the rails. The purpose of this chapter is to examine what went wrong, and to explain how monetary policy contributed to the financial crisis, drawing lessons that should enable policymakers to avoid repeating the same errors in future cycles. This is not to say that there were not other contributors to the crisis. In fact there were many, but monetary policy played a central role in laying the foundations for the asset price falls, the credit crunch and the subsequent recession.

Benign beginnings

From the time Britain abandoned the ERM in September 1992 until 2004 monetary policy in Britain was highly successful both in terms of achieving stable economic growth and in terms of maintaining low inflation. On the output side, real GDP growth averaged 2.8 per cent per annum and recorded positive growth in every single quarter between 1992 quarter three and 2008 quarter two. Unemployment declined steadily from its peak of 10.7 per cent in February 1993 to a low of 4.7 per cent by August 2004. A notable achievement during this period was that Britain avoided the recession that many countries experienced in the aftermath of the bursting of the dotcom bubble in 2000/01.

On the inflation side, retail and consumer prices remained within one percentage point of their assigned targets (initially 2.5 per cent for RPIX and later 2 per cent for the CPI). When the Bank of England was granted formal policy independence in 1997, this largely cemented the policy framework that had already been established, although there were numerous procedural and formal changes implemented under the 1998 Act.

The successful operation of monetary policy in the period 2000–04 can be attributed to three main elements. First, interest rates were adjusted with sufficient agility and sensitivity to arrange – deliberately or otherwise – that monetary growth did not become excessive. This can be demonstrated by reference to the growth of the broad money aggregate M4, which averaged 7.9 per cent per annum between 1997 and 2004, and 7.3 per cent per annum between 2000 and 2004. In practical terms this created headroom for roughly 3 per cent per annum real GDP growth combined with 2.5 per cent inflation and an average 1.5 per cent decline in income velocity every year.

Second, broader credit conditions remained similarly subdued. Between 1997 and 2004 the growth of debt owed by households, non-financial corporations, the government and financial institutions together (hereafter broad debt growth) averaged 8.6 per cent per annum, and only 6.7 per cent per annum between 2000 and 2004.

Third, after the dotcom bubble burst in 2000, the global economy remained considerably below full capacity utilisation rates, implying that from then until at least 2005 there was no capacity constraint tending to tighten supply–demand conditions and push up reported inflation rates.

Nevertheless numerous commentators, both from the Bank of England's own Monetary Policy Committee (MPC) and elsewhere, pointed to several undesirable developments in the UK and in the global economy during these years which caused concern. Foremost among these was the problem of the large-scale global imbalances, particularly the surpluses of the Asian economies and later the oil-producing economies. The large current account deficit of the UK was one of the more disturbing counterparts of this 'global savings glut'. Second, the continuing build-up of debt on household balance sheets in Britain was a regular topic of discussion, but not of policy.

Policy derailed

The year 2005 marked a critical turning point in UK monetary policy. In retrospect the most visible sign of this was the controversial decision of the MPC at its August meeting to cut interest rates from 4.75 per cent to 4.5 per cent. Although the vote was close (5–4), a focal point for the media was that the governor was outvoted. Much less visible was the start of a significant and sustained acceleration in M4 into double-digit growth rates, and an even steeper acceleration in the size of both financial sector balance sheets and the debt of the private non-financial corporate sector. These three developments together would combine to undermine the previous record of the Bank for stable conduct of monetary policy and financial stability, and ultimately created the building blocks for the crisis that developed in late 2007 and 2008.

Since the interest rate cut of August 2005 was the first critical mistake by the MPC it requires some more detailed examination. The background to the meeting, held three weeks after the terrorist bombings in central London, was that the Bank's repo rate had been kept unchanged at 4.75 per cent for a year since August 2004 following a series of rate hikes in 2003/04 from its low of 3.5 per cent in 2003.

Based on the MPC minutes, those who argued for no change in rates noted numerous signs of strength (or at least the lack of any imminent weakness). Such signals included the fact that equity prices in the FTSE All-Share index had risen by around 8 per cent since the May *Inflation Report*; that bank lending to private non-financial corporations had picked up; that oil prices were up 5 per cent over the month and 20 per cent since the May *Inflation Report*; that the economy was still operating close to full capacity; that services surveys were consistent with slightly stronger growth than in the official data; and that the money and credit data were consistent with a recovery in consumption and GDP growth in the second half of the year. Moreover, 'with oil prices likely to remain strong, producer input prices rising sharply, and an acceleration in unit labour costs ... it was too early to conclude that inflationary pressures had abated'.

On the other side of the debate, the fall in market interest rates compared with the flat yield curve at the time of the May *Inflation Report* implied that the market expected official interest rates to fall towards 4 per cent. The majority of members who voted for a cut preferred to focus on the subdued growth of output in the first half of the year, in particular household spending and business investment. They argued that high levels of household debt and the lagged impact of past interest rate increases accounted for some of the slowdown in consumer spending through 2004 and early 2005. They pointed to some slackening in the pressure of demand on supply capacity, which should lead to some moderation in inflation looking further ahead. A failure to reduce rates now might damage confidence. A cut in rates now would not preclude a rise in rates later if the data warranted it.

The committee's best collective judgement was that 'relative to the central projection, the balance of risks for activity was slightly to the downside in the near term. The balance of risks to inflation was correspondingly slightly on the downside further out'. In the event the vote was 5–4 for a cut of 0.25 per cent to 4.5 per cent. Given the delicate balance of evidence at the time it is perhaps not surprising that the decision was made to cut. What is surprising is that rates remained unchanged for another whole year, and were not raised again until August 2006.

In March 2005 M4 had shifted to double-digit growth rates for the first time since mid-1998. Furthermore, in the year that interest rates were kept unchanged until August 2006 the money growth rate accelerated steadily, rising to 13.3 per cent. Consequently, by the time the decision was made to raise rates in August 2006, M4 had already been growing at a double-digit pace for over a year and a half. Although official rates were subsequently raised from 4.75 per cent in August 2006, ultimately to a peak of 5.75 per cent in July 2007, M4 never decelerated significantly during this period. In fact growth rose further to reach a peak of 14.1 per cent in September 2007, and another interim peak of 13.9 per cent in May 2007, by which time CPI inflation had risen to 3.1 per cent (in March 2007). This led to the Governor having to write his first letter to the Chancellor of the Exchequer.

More broadly, financial market activity picked up substantially in the years after 2004, as evidenced in the dramatic growth of bank and non-bank financial sector balance sheet growth. Much of this surge in activity was based on financial innovations such as the process of securitisation whereby banks and investment banks packaged large numbers of mortgage loans or other loans into collateralised debt obligations (CDOs) or collateralised loan obligations (CLOs), 'sliced and diced' them into tranches of different credit quality (as assessed by the rating agencies), and then sold the CDO or CLO tranches to financial intermediaries such as Structured Investment Vehicles (SIVs), conduits, hedge funds or insurance companies and pension funds. Just taking loans drawn down by financial corporations, these increased from 71 per cent of GDP in 2002 to 129 per cent of GDP by early 2008. Using a broader definition of debt issued by the same financial corporations, total debt stood at 606 per cent of GDP in 2002, but by 2008 it had surged to 913 per cent of GDP. The overall increase in financial sector debt between 2002 and 2008 amounted to 90 per cent. Over the same period the market capitalisation of the financial sector in the FTSE All-Share index increased from 19.9 per cent in March 2000 to a peak of 31.4 per cent by January 2007.

Concluding lessons

There need be no problem with the growth of financial intermediation when it is broadly in line with the growth of the economy, or indeed when it is slightly faster than nominal GDP growth. In fact the tendency for income velocity to decline in many economies (i.e. for the money stock – which is the denominator in velocity – to grow slightly faster than nominal GDP) is the norm. The problem with *excessively* rapid growth of financial intermediation is that it necessarily implies there are substantial assets and liabilities building up both in the financial sector and in other sectors. Given the much lower growth of GDP, it is almost certain that either the asset values must significantly exceed their equilibrium values, predisposing the system to an asset price crash, and/or the liabilities are far in excess of the ability of the borrowers to service the debt on a sustainable basis, predisposing the system to an avalanche of debt defaults. This was the critical flaw in allowing M4 growth or broader financial sector debt growth to run so rampant for so long.

Throughout the period 2004–07 the record of MPC meetings shows that the members clearly underestimated the potential impact on inflation of rapid money growth. They also underestimated the impact on financial stability of overvalued asset prices (house prices, equities and commodities). Although they did discuss the growing accumulation of debt by the household sector and the releveraging of the non-financial corporate sector, they seldom discussed the question of what would happen to bank and financial sector balance sheets if securitised asset prices were to fall abruptly, or what might happen if credit growth slowed significantly from the excessive double-digit growth rates that their interest rate policy had permitted.

More fundamentally, the economic models used by the Bank almost certainly pay too little attention to vital parts of the transmission mechanism of monetary policy – namely the impact on the balance sheets of different sectors of a sustained period of excess money and credit growth, and the potential effect on the financial system and the economy as a whole of the unwinding of those excesses.

To close, it is worthwhile pondering this analogy. Between 1980 and 1985 the Bank of Japan pursued a monetary policy that called for stable growth of a monetary aggregate known as M2+CDs as an intermediate target for bringing down inflation. There was no specific inflation target, but stable money growth averaging 8.5 per cent over these years resulted in reasonably steady growth of real GDP averaging 3.3 per cent p.a. and low CPI inflation averaging 2.6 per cent p.a. between 1981 and 1986. In 1985 the Plaza Agreement and in 1987 the Louvre Accord derailed Japanese monetary policy, causing official interest rates to be lowered to 2.5 per cent and M2+CDs growth to accelerate from 8.5 per cent to an average of almost 11 per cent between 1987 and 1990 – figures remarkably similar to Britain's experience with M4 in 2004–08. The result was a disastrous asset bubble in 1985–90, followed by the bursting of that bubble from 1990 onwards. Arguably the Japanese economy has still not recovered from those mistakes of monetary policy.

In a numerical sense Governor King's Bank of England has closely replicated with M4 the Japanese experience with M2+CDs. It first replicated the experience of 1980–85 (for which much praise is due). But it then replicated the experience of 1987–90 with serious consequences. No doubt there are many differences between the two case studies, but as Mervyn King himself said on the eve of the crisis in May 2007, 'It is quite possible, in the real world, for there to be unwarranted money supply shocks – whether stimulus or restraint. The Monetary Policy Committee must always be looking for warning signals of this. The trap is falsely to conclude that, because some economic models contain no explicit reference to it, money cannot be one of those signals.'

Unfortunately, from 2005 onwards, the MPC failed to heed such warnings.

3 ORIGINS OF THE FINANCIAL MARKET CRISIS OF 2008

Anna J. Schwartz[1]

I begin by describing the factors that contributed to the financial market crisis of 2008. I end by proposing policies that could have prevented the baleful effects that produced the crisis.

Factors contributing to the crisis

At least three factors exercised significant influences on the emergence of the global financial crisis.

The basic groundwork to the disruption of credit flows can be traced to the asset price bubble of the housing boom. It has become a cliché to refer to an asset boom as a mania. The cliché, however, obscures why ordinary folk become avid buyers of whatever object has become the target of desire. An asset boom is propagated by an expansive monetary policy that lowers interest rates and induces borrowing beyond prudent bounds to acquire the asset.

The US Federal Reserve was accommodative too long from 2001 on and was slow to tighten monetary policy, delaying tightening until June 2004 and then ending the monthly 25 basis points increases in August 2006. The rate cuts that began on 10 August 2007 escalated to an unprecedented 75 basis points reduction on 22 January 2008, announced at an unscheduled video conference meeting a week before a scheduled Federal Open Market Committee meeting. The rate increases in 2007 were too little and ended too soon. This was the monetary policy setting for the housing price boom.

---

1   This chapter will appear as an article in the *Cato Journal*, 29(1), Winter 2009. It is reproduced by kind permission of the Cato Institute, Washington, DC, USA.

In the case of the housing price boom, the government played a role in stimulating demand for houses by proselytising the benefit of home ownership for the wellbeing of individuals and families. Congress was also more than a bit-part player in this campaign. Fannie Mae and Freddie Mac were created as government-sponsored enterprises. Beginning in 1992, Congress pushed Fannie Mae and Freddie Mac to increase their purchases of mortgages going to low- and moderate-income borrowers. In 1996, HUD, the department of Housing and Urban Development, gave Fannie Mae and Freddie Mac an explicit target: 42 per cent of their mortgage financing had to go to borrowers with incomes below the median income in their area. The target increased to 50 per cent in 2000 and 52 per cent in 2005. For 1996 HUD required that 12 per cent of all mortgage purchases by Fannie Mae and Freddie Mac had to be 'special affordable' loans, typically to borrowers with incomes less than 60 per cent of their area's median income. That number was increased to 20 per cent in 2000 and 22 per cent in 2005. The 2008 goal was to be 28 per cent. Between 2000 and 2005 Fannie Mae and Freddie Mac met those goals every year, and funded hundreds of billions of dollars' worth of loans, many of them sub-prime and adjustable-rate loans made to borrowers who bought houses with less than 10 per cent deposits. Fannie Mae and Freddie Mac also purchased hundreds of billions of sub-prime securities for their own portfolios to make money and help satisfy HUD affordable-housing goals. Fannie Mae and Freddie Mac were important contributors to the demand for sub-prime securities. Congress designed Fannie Mae and Freddie Mac to serve both their investors and the political class. Demanding that Fannie Mae and Freddie Mac do more to increase home ownership among poor people allowed Congress and the White House to subsidise low-income housing outside the budget, at least in the short run. Unfortunately, that strategy remains at the heart of the political process, and of proposed solutions to this crisis (Roberts, 2008). Fannie Mae and Freddie Mac were active politically, extending campaign contributions to legislators.

A further factor that influenced the emergence of the credit crisis was the adoption of innovations in investment instruments such as securiti-sation, derivatives and auction-rate securities before markets became aware of the flaws in the design of these instruments. The basic flaw in each of them was the difficulty of determining their price. Securitisation substituted the 'originate to distribute securities' model of mortgage lending in lieu of the traditional 'originate to hold mortgages' model. Additional banking innovations, notably the practices of the derivatives industry, made mortgage lending problems worse. Shifting risk is the basic property of derivatives. Risk was shifted in directions that became so complex, however, that neither the designers nor the buyers of these instruments apparently understood the risks they imposed and deriva-tive owners did not realise the risky contingencies they were assuming. Derivatives as well as mortgage-backed securities were difficult to price, an art that markets have not mastered. The securitisation of loans spread from the mortgage industry to commercial paper issuance, student loans, credit card receivables and other loan categories. The design of mortgage-backed securities collateralised by a pool of mortgages assumed that the pool would give the securities value. The pool, however, was an assort-ment of mortgages of varying quality. The designers gave no guidance on how to price the pool. They claimed that rating agencies would determine the price of the security. But the rating agencies had no formula for this task. They assigned ratings to complex securities as if they were ordinary corporate bonds and without examining the individual mortgages in the pool. Ratings tended to overstate the value of the securities and were fundamentally arbitrary. Without securitisation, all the various periph-eral players in the credit market debacle, including the bond insurers who unwisely insured securities linked to sub-prime mortgages, would not have been drawn into the subsidiary roles they exploited.

Securities and banking supervisors knew that the packaging of mortgage loans for resale as securities to investors was a threat to both investors and mortgage borrowers, but remained on the sidelines and made no attempt to halt the processes as they unfolded and transformed the mortgage market.

Another factor leading to the emergence of the credit crisis was the collapse of the market for some financial instruments. One particularly important instrument was the auction-rate security, a long-term instrument for which the interest rate is reset periodically at auctions. The instrument was introduced in 1984 as an alternative to long-term debt for borrowers who need long-term funding; but it serves as a short-term security. In 2007 outstanding auction-rate securities amounted to $330 billion. Normally, the periodic auctions give the bonds the liquidity of a short-term asset that trades at about par. The main issuers of auction-rate securities have been municipalities, hospitals, museums, student loan finance authorities and closed-end mutual funds. When an auction fails, there are fewer bidders than the number of securities to be sold. When this happens, the securities are priced at a penalty rate – typically, the state usury maximum, or a spread over LIBOR. This means the investor is unable to redeem his money and the issuer has to pay a higher rate to borrow.

Failed auctions were rare before the credit market crisis. The banks that conducted the auctions would inject their own capital to prevent an auction failure. From the autumn of 2007 on, these banks experienced credit losses and mortgage writedowns as a result of the sub-prime mortgage market collapse, and became less willing to commit their own money to keep auctions from failing. By February 2008 fears of such failures led investors to withdraw funds from the auction-rate securities market. The rate on borrowing costs rose sharply after failed auctions. The market became chaotic with different rates resulting for basically identical auction-rate securities. Different sectors have been distressed by the failure of the auction-rate securities market (Chicago Fed Letter, 2008).

The flaw in the design of this instrument has been revealed by its market collapse. A funding instrument that appears long-term to the borrower but short-term to the lender is an illusion. A funding instrument that *is* long-term for one party must be long-term for the counterparty. The auction-rate securities market is another example of ingenuity, similar to the brainstorm that produced securitisation. Each seemed to be a brilliant innovation. Securitisation produced products that were difficult to price. Auction-rate securities could not survive the inherent falsity of their conception. Both proved disastrous for credit market operations.

How to avoid a replay of the three factors that produced the credit market debacle

With respect to the first factor I have mentioned – the role of expansive monetary policy in propagating the housing price boom – let me first respond to Alan Greenspan's argument that no central bank could have terminated the asset price boom because, had it done so, the economy would have been engulfed in a recession that the public in a democracy would not stand for (Greenspan, 2008: Epilogue). The argument is fallacious. Greenspan does not explain why the Fed could not have conducted a less expansive monetary policy that did not lower interest rates to levels that made mortgage lending and borrowing appear riskless and encouraged house price increases. If monetary policy had been more restrictive, the asset price boom in housing could have been avoided

The second factor I suggested that led to the credit market debacle was the premature adoption of innovations in investment instruments that were flawed, principally because pricing the new instruments was difficult. Credit markets cannot operate normally if an accurate price cannot be assigned to the assets a would-be investor includes in his portfolio. The lesson for investors' embrace of mortgage-backed securities and other new types of assets that were profitable to many purveyors of services in the distribution of these ingenious ways of making loans is to be wary of innovations that have not been thoroughly tested.

The final factor that credit markets have contended with is the collapse of trading in selected instruments that revealed their weaknesses. The losses investors experienced as a result will keep these markets from operating until tranquillity returns to the credit market as a whole and the weaknesses have been corrected.

Much turmoil may still batter the credit markets. Capital impairment of banks and other financial firms remains to be dealt with. Insolvent firms must not be recapitalised with taxpayer funds. A systematic procedure for examining the portfolios of these institutions needs to be followed to identify which are insolvent.

References

Chicago Fed Letter (2008), 'Navigating the new world of private equity – a conference summary', *Chicago Fed Letter*, 256, November.

Greenspan, A. (2008), *The Age of Turbulence: Adventures in a New World*, New York: Penguin.

Roberts, R. (2008), 'How government stoked the mania', *Wall Street Journal*, 3 October.

4 THE FINANCIAL CRISIS: BLAME GOVERNMENTS, NOT BANKERS
Eamonn Butler

The popular story of the credit crisis runs like this.

Once upon a time, greedy bankers, mostly in the USA, made fortunes by selling mortgages to poor people who could not really afford them. They knew these loans were unsound, so they diced and sliced them and sold them in packages around the world to equally greedy bankers who did not know what they were buying. When the housing bubble burst, the borrowers defaulted, and bankers discovered that what they had bought was worthless. They went bust, business loans dried up, and the economy shuddered to a halt. The moral, according to this description of events, is that capitalism has failed, and we need tougher rules to curb bankers' greed and make sure all this never happens again.

The story is popular because there is much truth in it. The crisis did start in the USA. US lenders did lend to people who were not credit-worthy, and they did package and sell on their bad, 'sub-prime' business. Bankers did buy these infected packages, and did run out of cash. And yes, there has been a lot of greed and stupidity within commercial firms.

What is missing from the story, however, is the fact that all of these crimes, follies and misfortunes stem from government action. Their causes are political intervention in the mortgage and banking markets, wild extravagance by the official monetary authorities, and unfocused and inept government regulators.

The deep roots of the crisis

The real story has roots going back to the last great financial crisis, the 1930s Great Depression. Credit was tight; mortgages were hard to get, houses were not selling, and the building industry was collapsing. So the government stepped in to try to revive the market and boost lenders' confidence.

Various new agencies were created, among them the Federal Housing Administration (FHA), which guaranteed the banks' mortgage risks, and the Federal National Mortgage Association (FNMA or Fannie Mae), which effectively insured mortgages by being prepared to buy them from lenders. These federal guarantees passed risk from the lenders – principally the Savings & Loan (S&L) institutions (akin to Britain's building societies) – to the US taxpayer.

The US government also intervened deeply in lenders' operations. The Glass-Steagall Act of 1933 allowed the Federal Reserve to set limits on the rates that banks could pay their depositors (Regulation Q). The S&Ls benefited because they had no such limits. But the S&Ls were also restricted to long-term mortgage business, so they were in the potentially risky position of being committed to financing 30-year loans while their savers could move their deposits at short notice.

Sharp and volatile rises in interest rates in the late 1960s and 1970s meant the S&Ls did indeed face difficulties as depositors took out their cash to put into higher-rate savings vehicles elsewhere. By the early 1980s, the S&Ls were technically insolvent. Congress deregulated, but too late: by 1995 the number of S&Ls had halved to just 1,645. Two other 1930s government creations, the Federal Savings & Loan Insurance Corporation (FSLIC) and the Federal Deposit Insurance Corporation (FDIC), picked up the bill, at a cost of $150 billion to US taxpayers.

This long catalogue of government intervention stopped the mortgage market working properly. Competition was restricted. Regulation prevented institutions from adapting to market conditions. Bad loans, and bad business decisions, were underwritten by taxpayers.

How politicians forced bankers to make bad loans

The final ingredient in this poisonous cocktail was the Community Reinvestment Act (CRA), which President Jimmy Carter signed on 13 October 1977. Its aim was laudable – to promote home ownership for minorities. It made illegal the practice of redlining, whereby lenders would simply refuse mortgages in poor (and commonly black and Hispanic) areas on the grounds that low-quality housing and high levels of unemployment and welfare dependency made local residents unattractive as borrowers.

From now on, the lenders were expected to conduct business over the whole of the geographical area they served. They could not favour the suburbs over the inner-city districts. To make sure they complied, the 1975 Home Mortgage Disclosure Act (HMDA) forced lenders to provide detailed reports about whom they lent to. And the Carter administration also funded various 'community' groups, such as the Association of Community Organisations for Reform Now (ACORN), to help monitor their performance on the CRA rules.

In 1991 the HMDA rules were strengthened to include a specific demand for racial equality in the institutions' lending. In 1992 the Federal Reserve Bank of Boston published a manual for lenders that went even further. It advised them that a mortgage applicant's lack of credit history should not be seen as a negative factor in assessing them for a loan; that lenders should not flinch if borrowers used loans or gifts for their mortgage deposit; and that unemployment benefits would be a valid source of income for lending decisions. It also reminded them that failing to meet CRA regulations could be a violation of equal opportunity laws that exposed them to actual damages plus punitive damages of $500,000.

The government went further, 'streamlining' the CRA regulations in 1995 to allow, and indeed force, lenders to ignore most of the traditional criteria of creditworthiness in their loan decisions. Mortgages could now be any multiple of income; a person's saving history was irrelevant; applicants' income did not need to be verified; and participation in a credit counselling programme could be taken as proof of an applicant's ability to manage a loan. In other words, the government was now forcing the institutions to make loans to people who they knew were not creditworthy.

And to make sure all this happened, more taxpayer funds were given to monitoring groups such as ACORN. As public scrutiny of bank mergers and acquisitions increased following their 1994 Riegle-Neal deregulation, these groups were actually able to hold the banks to ransom. Under the CRA, if a lender wants to change its business operation in any way – merging with another bank, opening or closing branches, or developing new products – it must convince the regulators that it will continue to make sufficient loans to the government's preferred groups of borrowers. ACORN and others can file petitions with the regulators to stop the banks' plans.

Bad loans and booming markets

Not surprisingly, the banks paid the ransom. And now that creditworthiness was no longer a requirement for getting a loan, the number of sub-prime loans boomed. Home ownership increased, from 65 per cent of households to 69 per cent between 1995 and 2004, representing about 4.6 million new homeowners. This put pressure on house prices, which also rose sharply from their stable position in the early 1990s.

Meanwhile, a 1992 law was pushing the government-sponsored Fannie Mae and its younger twin the Federal Home Loan Mortgage Company (Freddie Mac) to devote more effort to meeting wider home ownership goals. High-risk loans were everywhere. Even the FHA promoted more credit to poor borrowers by offering low-deposit loans. And Freddie Mac actually developed the process of securitising bad loan packages and selling this bad debt around the world. This business boomed after 1995 too.

Fannie and Freddie profited from this system, while passing most of the risk on to taxpayers. To make sure, they contributed heavily to congressional offices, and spent hundreds of millions on lobbying and pressure groups. Other unscrupulous lenders also knew that Freddie and Fannie – and ultimately the taxpayers – would guarantee their bad loans, so were happy to make more of them.

While house prices continued to rise, everything seemed to go well. Even the riskiest borrowers were meeting their payments. Some people refinanced on the back of rising house prices and pocketed nice profits. And other government interventions kept the bubble growing. Land-use regulations, limiting the opportunity for house building, pushed prices up further. Income tax deductions for mortgages favoured housing over other savings.

Meanwhile, the Federal Reserve – assisted by the Bank of England – had flooded world markets with credit after the stock market crash of 1987. They did the same again whenever any downturn threatened – the dotcom crash, and spectacularly after 9/11, when interest rates came down from 6.25 per cent to just 1 per cent – which just boosted borrowing even more. So house prices continued their rise, and home-owners enjoyed the boom.

There seemed every reason to buy houses, and no reason not to. By 2006, perhaps a fifth of buyers were simply speculators – not just middle-class speculators, but low-income ones too. In states like California, where lenders could not go after a borrower's assets, there was no risk at all: if things went wrong, you simply sent the keys back to the lender and walked away. They called it 'jingle mail'.

The inevitable bust

But in 2006 the bubble burst. It had to as it was inflated to bursting point by the Federal Reserve's loose monetary policy. House prices collapsed, and borrowers defaulted. A year later the banks realised what poor-quality securities they had bought. Despite having 236 regulators on their case, Fannie and Freddie – guarantors of half of US mortgages – plunged into massive deficit and collapsed.

It was a boom, and a bust, made entirely by government. And the boom and bust in Britain had many of the same features and causes. Gordon Brown's continual reassurances that the era of boom and bust was over made us believe that the boom we experienced was real, and desensitised us to the risk of collapse. House prices spiralled upwards; people again refinanced and took the profits of rising prices; others bought buy-to-let homes speculatively; and the green belt and other planning restrictions kept the supply of homes low while immigration from the new EU members put increasing pressure on demand.

But monetary policy was not focused on reining in this credit boom. Indeed, Gordon Brown changed the price index that the Bank of England was to target to the Consumer Prices Index (CPI). This excludes housing costs, unlike the Retail Prices Index, so the soaring cost of housing was not taken into account by the Monetary Policy Committee (MPC). At the same time, China and other developing countries were producing tradable goods more cheaply, so CPI growth remained relatively low. Eventually, of course, the MPC had problems meeting even its 2 per cent price-growth target. Like the Federal Reserve, the Bank had stoked up a huge inflation.

When Gordon Brown gave the Bank independence on monetary policy, he also shifted its role in bank regulation to the new Financial Services Authority (FSA). But the Bank had a better grasp of what was happening in the markets. Its roles in setting interest rates and acting as lender of last resort were complementary to its former role of regulating banks. The FSA proved it could not keep up with the fast-moving world of derivatives and credit swaps.

The Bank of England warned the FSA that Northern Rock was operating riskily in October 2006, long before it collapsed; but no effective action was taken. When Northern Rock's problems surfaced, the old-style Bank of England would never have allowed it to open for business the next Monday until its problems were fixed. But Northern Rock opened, and the sight of thousands of depositors queuing to remove their funds prompted the Chancellor to bail it out. And having guaranteed the riskiest lender, the government could not stand by, months later, when other banks got into difficulty – so yet more taxpayers' money was put at risk.

International regulation compounded the problems. The Basel II rules focused on capital, rather than the immediate problem when the mortgage bubble burst, which was liquidity. Banks found themselves having to sell assets in a falling market to keep their margins up. Indeed, arguably, international capital regulations may well have made the problem worse.

The moral: it's government failure, not market failure

Now the world's politicians are telling us that we need more financial regulation to save us from the failures of capitalism. But the moral of this story is that the crisis actually represents a vast failure of government. Its causes are a catalogue of political, legislative and regulatory failures going back for decades. Where there has been greed and ineptitude, by banks or by borrowers, it has been able to flourish only in the unreal boom world that government action created.

We have been in a casino where the government was handing out free chips and the regulators were buying drinks and telling us which numbers to bet on. Not surprisingly, we have all left poorer than we went in.

Bibliography

DiLorenzo, T. J. (2008), 'The CRA scam and its defenders', Ludwig von Mises Institute Daily Article, www.mises.org/story/2963.

Liebowitz, S. J. (2008), 'Anatomy of a train wreck: causes of the mortgage meltdown', Independent Institute Policy Report, www.independent.org/pdf/policy_reports/2008-10-03-trainwreck.pdf.

Utt, R. D. (2008), 'The best red tape your tax money can buy', Heritage Foundation Press Commentary, www.heritage.org/Press/Commentary/ed103108d.cfm.

Utt, R. D. (2008), 'The subprime mortgage market collapse: a primer on the causes and possible solutions', Heritage Foundation Backgrounder 2127, www.heritage.org/Research/Economy/bg2127.cfm.

5 MARKET FOUNDATIONS FOR THE NEW FINANCIAL ARCHITECTURE
Michael Beenstock

Market economics is on trial. Many are arguing that the financial crisis has been induced by market failure and that recent experiments with financial deregulation made the sub-prime crisis inevitable. They are calling for stronger and more effective regulation.[1] My thesis is that regulation is part of the problem rather than its solution. The regulatory paradigm upon which the old financial architecture was designed, and which has dominated thinking since Bagehot, has failed and the time has come to replace it. The solution lies instead in founding the New Financial Architecture on the 'information paradigm', which calls for greater transparency in reporting by financial institutions, and which recognises that financial markets in particular cannot function properly without adequate information. It also calls for minimal regulation, or even no regulation at all.

Information runs

Under the regulatory paradigm, financial institutions report to their regulators but not to the public. Banks provide regulators with detailed information on their loan portfolios. Since these data are not published the public cannot make informed judgements about the risk exposure of individual banks. Even if the data were published it would be difficult to form judgements about the quality of bank credit because the laws of confidentiality prevent naming individual bank clients. It would make a great deal of difference, however, if data at least on the sectoral

---

1   See, for example, De Grauwe (2008) and Eichengreen and Baldwin (2008).

composition of the loan portfolios of individual banks were made public. The public would then know the involvement of individual banks in, say, mortgages, construction and many other credit sectors, where downside risk may be particularly large.[2]

Suppose a solvency problem arises in a specific credit sector, such as mortgages, and bank A is heavily exposed in this sector, while other banks are not exposed. At present the public has no way of knowing whether the same problem applies in banks B, C, etc. This triggers a run on these banks because the public fears incorrectly that they might be insolvent too. It is in this way that a solvency crisis for one bank turns into a liquidity crisis for all banks and indeed for the financial system as a whole.[3] Had the public had access to information on the credit exposures of the individual banks, depositors would have understood that only bank A has a solvency problem. They would have transferred their deposits from bank A to other banks and there would have been no run on the banking system as a whole. In the absence of deposit insurance some of the depositors would have lost their money. But this is no different in principle from losses that are incurred when any business goes bankrupt.

Just as the public has no information, nor do the banks themselves. Banks B and C suspect that other banks might be insolvent like bank A, and refuse to lend to each other in the interbank market. Since the same applies to banks D, E, etc., the entire interbank market collapses. What started as a simple insolvency problem for bank A rapidly turns into a financial pandemic simply because information on bank portfolios is withheld from the public. The collapse of the interbank market triggers a credit crunch, which in turn leads to further insolvency, and so the information run enters another round. For want of a nail the kingdom was lost.

---

2   The seminal model in Diamond and Dybvig (1983) and Diamond (1984) assumes that all debtor heterogeneity is unobservable. Since systematic risk varies across credit sectors, however, much of the heterogeneity is observable. See Beenstock and Khatib (2008).

3   The theory of 'information runs' is discussed by Jacklin and Bhattacharya (1988), which should be distinguished from the theory of 'sunspot runs' of Diamond and Dybvig (1983).

Had banks known in advance that information about their exposures would become public knowledge they would have acted differently and with greater caution. They would not have lent in particularly risky sectors for fear of punishment by the market. House prices are inherently cyclical and volatile because the time to build is long and because houses are long-lived assets.[4] As house prices climbed towards their peak bankers should have exercised caution by reducing their mortgage exposure in the face of increasing downside risk in the housing market. They had no incentive to act cautiously, however, because only the regulator was provided with the relevant information. Through long experience bankers know that regulators do not behave punitively. Even moments before the ship went down banks were selling 100-per-cent-plus mortgages to people who could not afford them.

Not only do banks face incentives to act incautiously, they face incentives to skimp on capital and to become over-leveraged. Bankers know that in the event of need they will be bailed out. Therefore regulation induces a double moral hazard; banks take more risk and they hold less capital.

Regulatory failure

In the post-mortem following the financial crisis, regulatory failure should be put under the spotlight. Why did regulators, who had access to all the relevant information, fail in their task? The answer lies in public choice or 'capture' theory.[5] Just as the incentives facing the regulated are unhealthy, so are the incentives facing the regulators. There are two aspects to this. First, like other human beings regulators enjoy power. Keynes remarked that there is nothing more exhilarating to central bankers than a fully blown financial crisis. They move to centre

---

4   Sharp increases in house prices are typically mistaken for bubbles. See Bar-Nathan et al. (1998).

5   'Capture' theory, originally developed by Stigler (1970) and Posner (1974), predicts that regulators become the captives of the regulated instead of agents of the public good.

stage and become the focus of public attention as they save the world. Regulators have an incentive, therefore, to regulate; they have a self-interest in allowing problems to develop. While this may be a motivation for senior managers, at other levels in a regulatory authority those responsible for regulating institutions have an incentive not to bring emerging problems to public attention. If a solvency problem arises, the responsible regulator might be regarded as having underperformed in his job. Thus, the regulator has an incentive to wait and hope that market movements will resolve the problem. Whatever the motivation, financial regulators tend to have incentives to delay acting.

Second, regulators do not remain regulators for ever. Regulators eventually pass through the 'revolving door' to good jobs in the regulated sector and vice versa. They therefore do not want to jeopardise their future careers by being too hard on their quarries. Gamekeepers turn poachers. This double-edged moral hazard makes regulatory failure inevitable. Of course, bankers internalise this and play their part in the regulation game. They take risks in the knowledge that their regulators will turn a blind eye. In short, as Kane (1997) and Benston (1998) point out, there is an 'agency problem' in financial regulation since regulators do not act as agents of the public at large. They act instead in their own self-interest and in the interests of the regulated.

Providing regulators with information on credit exposures is therefore not the same thing as providing this information to the public. Imagine what would happen if the same non-disclosure rules applied to non-financial companies, which reported only to their regulators and did not publish financial reports as required by law. The public would have no information with which to make informed judgements about the market value of public companies. A solvency problem in one company could lead to a liquidity crisis in other companies. The regulator would then be called in to prevent a run on the business sector. This nightmare does not happen thanks to the onus of company reporting and the development of accounting standards. Indeed, prior to the development of the joint stock company in the nineteenth century and disclosure requirements, stock markets were prone to instability and manipulation owing to lack of information.

What applies to banks also applies to other financial institutions such as insurance companies and investment banks, which should be required to disclose their asset compositions. These institutions do not need regulators. Suppose, for example, that Lehman Brothers had published its exposure in the US mortgage market and that the Royal Bank of Scotland (RBS) had published its holdings of bonds issued by Lehman Brothers. The public and financial analysts would have understood that RBS was exposing itself indirectly to US mortgage risk, and that Lehman Brothers was adding risk to its portfolio. Maybe the rating agencies would also have done a better job[6] instead of continuing to grant AAA ratings to Lehman Brothers and RBS. The discipline of information transparency would have made both institutions behave more cautiously in the first place and it would have nipped the sub-prime crisis in the bud.

In summary, the regulatory paradigm as applied to banks is fundamentally flawed. This paradigm, which has been adopted in all countries, has been responsible for intermittent financial instability. Until it is understood that the root cause of financial instability lies in information theory, the world will continue to suffer from periodic financial instability.

Recent proposals[7] to generate a system of global regulation under the auspices of a World Financial Organisation, which would set rules for global finance, are based on a fundamental conceptual error. It is ironic that commentators such as Joseph Stiglitz and Michael Spence, who were awarded the Nobel Prize in Economics for their work on asymmetric information theory, have failed to appreciate the significance of their own scientific contributions. It is also ironic that Ben Bernanke,

---

6   This does not exonerate rating agencies for receiving payments from the companies that they were rating, though this issue is covered in greater detail in the chapter by Morrison.

7   These proposals were made even before the outbreak of the current crisis. See, e.g., Eichengreen (1999), Bryant (2003) and Roubini and Uzan (2006).

who did so much to apply asymmetric information theory to banking, has done the same. Stiglitz and Weiss (1981) established that asymmetric information induces credit rationing. Indeed, credit crunching is predicted by asymmetric information theory. There will always be irreducible asymmetric information because creditors can never fully know what motivates debtors. The vast majority of asymmetric information is reducible, however, because regulators treat the information that they have as if it were nuclear secrets. The asymmetry is artificially induced because regulators refuse to reveal to the public the very information that would prevent bank runs and credit crunches.

Evidence

It is no coincidence that the financial institutions that have got into difficulty are almost exclusively regulated. To the best of my knowledge unregulated offshore banks have thus far survived the financial crisis. Indeed, this may be surprising to some since depositors are often warned that offshore banks are dangerous because they are unregulated, do not have a lender of last resort, and face no restrictions on capital adequacy or liquidity. It is precisely because offshore banks are unregulated that they are more stable. Since they have nobody to bail them out, they cannot afford to behave incautiously. They do not skimp on capital and liquidity and cannot afford to participate in financial adventures, because, unlike onshore banks, they have no regulation game to play. Benston (1998) notes, 'Before depositors relied on government for protection, banks maintained much more substantial capital/asset ratios; in fact, banks used to advertise prominently the amount of their capital and surplus.'

It is also no coincidence that the sub-prime crisis originated in the US mortgage market. Fannie Mae and Freddie Mac are two politicised institutions whose mission since 1992 was to promote home ownership. They could raise cheap capital in the bond market because it was understood that they had semi-official backing, as was subsequently proved correct. They were especially encouraged to target low-income families who received mortgages that they could not afford, so that politicians could boast about the spread of home ownership in their constituencies. In Germany too, where there was no increase in house prices, the troublesome banks were either state-owned (Länderbanks) or politicised (IKB bank). When these banks got into difficulty an information run was triggered on private banks. Good German banks were brought down with the bad. Politics and stable banking do not mix.[8]

It will be asked how the collapse of US investment banks and insurance companies is consistent with my thesis. After all, Bear Stearns, Lehman Brothers and AIG were unregulated like their offshore counterparts. The answer lies in 'regulatory creep'. The Savings & Loans (S&L) crisis in the 1980s was very much a forerunner to the current US mortgage crisis. S&Ls financed fixed-interest-rate mortgages through equity and deposits insured by the Federal Savings and Loan Insurance Corporation (FSLIC) and regulated by the Federal Home Loan Bank Board. When US interest rates rose in 1978–81, three-quarters of the S&Ls became insolvent and FSLIC became insolvent too. The bailout of the S&Ls cost taxpayers $150 billion. Long Term Capital Management (LTCM), the hedge fund that was bailed out in 1998, was unregulated. The writing was on the wall. If LTCM was bailed out, why should other unregulated financial institutions not be bailed out too? Against the backdrop of the S&L bailout, the bailout of LTCM created a moral hazard problem in unregulated financial institutions.

Something similar happened in the UK when in 1985 Johnson-Matthey Bankers was bailed out by the Bank of England despite the fact that it was a very small unregulated bank with no economic significance beyond the gold market. The Bank of England was quick to panic, and feared an information run on the large retail banks. Managers of unregulated financial institutions are increasingly operating in a climate

---

8　The banking crisis in Israel in 1983 could not have happened without the cooperation of regulators at the Bank of Israel. The Supervisor of Banks at the time of the crash became the CEO of Bank Leumi.

of moral hazard since they know that if necessary they will benefit from 'regulation creep' and regulators will save them even if they are unregulated. This moral hazard has been greatly increased by the massive bailouts in the current crisis. The seeds have been planted for the next financial crisis as the regulation game is played out even among financial institutions that are unregulated.

Since financial institutions have been regulated for so long, one has to look elsewhere to learn how the information paradigm might function. Prior to the Life Assurance Companies Act 1870 the life insurance industry had an unstable and poorly defined legal framework and the industry was often plagued by instability. The 1870 Act defined a broadly liberal regulatory framework, certainly in comparison with those that existed overseas, which simply required companies to publish information under the so-called 'freedom with publicity' policy.[9] This augured 100 years of stability and growth in the industry. This policy came to an end when the UK joined the EU and was required to enforce its regulatory framework. The 1870 Act essentially applied the information paradigm and what had been a regulated but unstable industry was transformed into a deregulated but stable industry subsequently. The crucial ingredient of the Act was information disclosure to the market, which enabled actuaries to value and pass opinions on companies and which restrained companies from overexposure to risk on both sides of the balance sheet.

Principles of financial misregulation

To justify financial regulation, Brunnermeier et al. (2009) list five negative banking externalities, all of which are false. The first is informational contagion; if bank A fails this will cast doubt on the solvency of other banks. I have already disposed of the argument. The second is that if customers of bank A transfer their business to bank B, loan officers in B will know less about the credit risk of these customers than loan officers

---

9   See Booth (2007) for a history of the 'freedom with publicity' policy.

in A. This imaginary externality is not limited to banks, and in any case bank B may obtain information on their new customers from credit risk companies. Third, they claim that negative externalities arise through the interbank market. This market is simply an example of inter-industry trade. The existence of inter-industry trade has never been mooted as a source of negative externality. Therefore if bank A does business with bank B, there is no more reason why bank B should fail just because A and B happen to be banks rather than breweries. If, however, non-financial corporations behaved like banks by failing to provide the public with information, we would see 'brewery runs' as well as bank runs.

Fourth, if bank A sells assets to raise liquidity asset prices will fall and the balance sheets of other banks will be adversely affected. Brunnermeier et al. see this as their major new contribution to the theory of systemic risk and financial regulation. But how can an individual bank affect asset prices when it holds but a tiny fraction of the stock of assets in the market? In any case, this imaginary externality would apply universally and not just to banks. Their fifth externality is equally imaginary. If bank A fails, a contraction of credit will be induced with adverse macroeconomic consequences. The macroeconomic implications of a bank failure are not inherently different to those of a brewery failure, provided banks like breweries keep the public informed. In one case there may be less credit and in the other less beer.

I have taken Brunnermeier et al. as a representative example of woolly thinking. One might just as easily invent a theory of brewery regulation as a theory of financial regulation. Banks and financial corporations are not inherently different. They seem different only because banks do not supply the public with sufficient information and banks have regulators while breweries do not.

The future

The regulation paradigm that underpinned the Old Financial Architecture has completely broken down. The idea that clever global regulators and whistle-blowers can ensure financial stability in the future is an expression of intellectual despair. We are currently witnessing an epidemic of desperate advice: if the paradigm has failed it must be because it was not applied correctly. These desperate voices call to strengthen regulation, make it more watertight and globalise it. Stiglitz is even suggesting that a world currency, based on Keynes's bancor, be introduced with a world central bank to operate it.

These are signs that the regulatory paradigm is in its death throes. I am suggesting that the new paradigm be based on information theory, which should serve as the market foundations of the New Financial Architecture. A practical starting point for this public disclosure policy should be the reporting requirements under Pillar 3 of Basel II, which *inter alia* requires banks to report value at risk (VaR). Indeed, Pillar 3 is based on the principle that market discipline will be enhanced if banks publish information on credit risk by economic branch, as well as information on impaired loans. Under the information paradigm banks and other financial businesses will have an incentive to be transparent and to disclose information. Just as commercial businesses have an incentive to extol the virtues of their products, so will financial businesses have an incentive to persuade the public that their deposits etc. are safe. Indeed, disclosure will generate a genuine industry in the rating of financial products, which in principle is no different to the widespread rating of commercial products.

Derivatives have existed since time immemorial. Following theoretical breakthroughs in the 1970s in the pricing of derivatives, however, the market in financial derivatives has expanded enormously. Derivatives, including credit default swaps (CDS), are instruments providing insurance services and which fulfil an important social function. Since they mitigate risk they encourage business. Genuine hedge funds[10] ensure that derivative prices are at their competitive levels. In the New Financial

---

10   Hedge portfolios have no wealth since they are long in the derivative and short in the fundamental asset. Many so-called hedge funds are not hedge funds at all because they do not hedge their positions.

Architecture hedge funds must be allowed to short sell, otherwise they cannot fulfil their market function (see the chapter by Copeland).

It is falsely argued that the provision of lender-of-last-resort (LOLR) insurance justifies regulation to prevent moral hazard. Insurance companies deal with moral hazard through deductibles and no-claims bonuses which provide incentives for the insured to behave cautiously, thereby eliminating most if not all of the moral hazard. To internalise moral hazard, Bagehot insisted in *Lombard Street* that banks be penalised for claiming LOLR insurance.[11] The New Financial Architecture will greatly reduce the need for LOLR insurance because information runs will be rarer. The need will not, however, be entirely eliminated. Shareholders should be made to internalise LOLR moral hazard by paying deductibles, a precedent for which may be found in the British government's recent treatment of shareholders of the Royal Bank of Scotland.[12] This principle should be extended to CEOs since agency problems in corporate governance mean that they too should have a direct interest in internalising moral hazard. This feature of the New Financial Architecture would further reduce the need for regulation. Since regulation induces moral hazard, the New Financial Architecture should do without regulation altogether.

In summary, the main structures of the New Financial Architecture are:

1. Banks should make public the sectoral composition of their credit portfolio under Pillar 3 of Basel II.
2. Banks should make public value at risk under Pillar 3 of Basel II.
3. Shareholders and CEOs should pay deductibles when claiming LOLR insurance.
4. Bank regulation should cease.

---

11 Bagehot was also aware that LOLR insurance would induce banks to skimp on liquidity and capital. He was not apparently aware that moral hazard would also induce banks to take on more risk.

12 Though, in this case, it can be a private arrangement between the central bank and the banks that may wish to make use of LOLR functions.

5. Similar principles should be applied to investment banks and insurance companies.
6. Hedge funds should be allowed to short sell.
7. Credit rating agencies should declare whether they have been paid by rated companies.

Economic history is replete with examples when quite simple concepts, unknown to politicians and their advisers, induce economic havoc. When Britain left the gold standard in 1931 Ramsay MacDonald apparently never knew that it was morally or technically possible to float the exchange rate. When in 1976 James Callaghan abandoned incomes policy and Keynesian demand management theory in favour of monetarism, he did not apparently know that there was an alternative paradigm to Keynesianism. The same applies today. There is an alternative to the regulatory paradigm whose intellectual roots lie in information theory. Financial markets are not endemically unstable. Society does not have to put up with intermittent financial crises. Politicians need to be informed of the information paradigm before designing the New Financial Architecture.

References

Bar Nathan, M., M. Beenstock and Y. Haitovsky (1998), 'The market for housing in Israel', *Regional Science and Urban Economics*, 28: 21–50.

Beenstock, M. and M. Khatib (2008), 'Contagion and correlation in empirical factor models of bank credit risk', www.huji.ac.il/economics/beenstock.

Benston, G. J. (1998), *Regulating Financial Markets: A Critique and Some Proposals*, Hobart Paper 135, London: Institute of Economic Affairs.

Booth, P. (2007), '"Freedom with publicity" – the actuarial profession and United Kingdom insurance regulation from 1844 to 1945', *ASA*, 2: 114–45.

Brunnermeier, M., A. Crocket, C. Goodhart, A. Persaud and H. Shin (2009), *The Fundamental Principles of Financial Regulation*, Geneva Reports on the World Economy 11.

Bryant, R. (2003), *Turbulent Waters: Cross-Border Finance and International Governance*, Washington, DC: Brookings Institution.

De Grauwe, P. (2008), 'The banking crisis: causes, consequences and remedies', University of Leuven, November.

Diamond, D. (1984), 'Financial intermediation and delegated monitoring', *Review of Economic Studies*, 51: 393–414.

Diamond, D. and P. Dybvig (1983), 'Bank runs, liquidity and deposit insurance', *Journal of Political Economy*, 91: 401–19.

Eichengreen, B. (1999), *Towards a New International Financial Architecture: A Practical Post-Asia Agenda*, Washington, DC: Institute for International Economics.

Eichengreen, B. and R. Baldwin (2008), *What G20 Leaders Must Do to Stabilize Our Economy and Fix the Financial System*, www.voxeu.org/index.php?q=node/2543.

Jacklin, C. J. and S. Bhattacharya (1988), 'Distinguishing panics and information-based bank runs: welfare and policy implications', *Journal of Political Economy*, 91: 568–92.

Kane, E. J. (1997), 'Ethical foundations of financial regulation', *Journal of Financial Accounting Research*, 1: 13–29.

Posner, R. A. (1974), 'Theories of economic regulation', *Bell Journal of Economics and Management Science*, 5: 337–52.

Roubini, N. and M. Uzan (eds) (2006), *New International Financial Architecture*, Cheltenham: Edward Elgar.

Stigler, G. J. (1970), 'The theory of economic regulation', *Bell Journal of Economics and Management Science*, 2: 3–21.

Stiglitz, J. E. and A. M. Weiss (1981), 'Credit rationing in markets with imperfect information', *American Economic Review*, 73: 339–410.

6 THE FAILURE OF CAPITAL ADEQUACY REGULATION
Kevin Dowd

Capital adequacy regulation is a relatively new development in modern central banking. It can be traced to the establishment of the Basel Committee in 1974 to provide a basis for international cooperation in bank supervision. The work of the Basel Committee soon focused on setting international standards of capital adequacy regulation – that is to say, on the stipulation of minimum regulatory capital requirements for banks – the main purpose of which is to ensure that banks have enough capital to absorb prospective losses with a very high probability and still remain solvent. The Basel Capital Accord then followed in 1988. The original Accord has been revised several times and the latest version, Basel II, came into effect in January 2008. Similar regulations have also been applied to other financial institutions, most notably the Solvency I and Solvency II systems regulating the capital adequacy of insurance companies in the EU. Since the Basel Committee was first established, the scope and especially the scale of capital adequacy regulation have grown enormously. One is, however, tempted to suggest that its effectiveness is in inverse proportion to its amount.

Rationale

Capital adequacy regulation can be assessed using three different criteria: its *rationale*, its *process*, and the *rules* and *their effects*. Beginning with the first of these, this regulation is often justified by its proponents in terms of paternalistic philosophies of public policy (e.g., that it is allegedly necessary to protect bank depositors or borrowers) or in terms of external effect considerations. It is also sometimes justified as countering the moral hazard problems created by deposit insurance (see, for example, Benston and Kaufman, 1986), which effectively amounts to saying that we need one form of government intervention to counter the problems created by another. There have, however, been very few attempts to justify capital adequacy regulation on economic first principles by reference to a market failure that capital adequacy regulation can somehow 'correct'.

A notable exception is an argument by David Miles (1995). The essence of his argument is that *if* depositors cannot assess the financial soundness of individual banks, then banks will maintain lower-than-optimal capital ratios, where the optimal capital ratios are those that banks would have observed if depositors could have assessed their financial positions properly. Miles's solution is for a regulator to assess the level of capital the bank would have maintained in the absence of the information asymmetry and then force it to maintain this level of capital. This argument is, however, open to the objection that under historical systems of relatively limited regulation depositors generally had little difficulty assessing the quality of their banks' assets (see, for example, Kaufman, 1987). The logic of this argument also runs into a dilemma. *If* the information exists (or could exist) for the regulator to formulate a feasible capital adequacy rule, that *same* information could presumably *also* be used to convey credible signals to depositors about the capital strength of their banks and thereby enable them to distinguish one bank's capital strength from another's (for more on this argument, see Dowd, 1999.) In this case, the capital adequacy regulation is not needed. But if that information *cannot* be collected, on the other hand, then the regulator cannot collect it either, and in that case Miles's capital adequacy regulation is not feasible. Either way, there is no market failure for the central bank to 'correct'.

Process

We can also assess capital adequacy regulation in terms of the process that produces it. Capital regulations emanate from a highly politicised international committee process, and are the product of arbitrary decisions, irrational compromises and much political horse-trading. They also reflect the personalities and prejudices of the main participants involved, and Basel insiders talk of intense political pressures, tight deadlines, high stress and stand-up rows. This process almost inevitably leads to rules that are poorly thought through (e.g. inconsistent treatment, regulatory arbitrage opportunities and so on), a compliance culture and onerous implementation costs. Over time, it also leads to ever longer rule books that attempt to standardise approaches in an area where practice is always changing and where the development of best practice requires competition in risk management systems – not an irrelevant and inflexible rule book that is out of date before it comes out.

It is also a curious paradox that though the regulations are signed off by the committees that produce them, individual members of those committees are notoriously reluctant to defend them when speaking on their own account: it is as if everyone understands that the rules are indefensible and is too embarrassed to defend them, but they still feel obliged to sign up to the group-think process that produces them. In fact, I have never met a regulator or former regulator who was privately willing to defend the regulatory rule book. Another aspect of this same paradox is that the proponents of capital adequacy regulation are willing to defend it only in principle, but not in terms of its concrete reality. In this context, in his book *Plight of the Fortune Tellers* (2007), Riccardo Rebonato tells a nice anecdote from a big risk management conference in 2005. He quotes an unnamed 'very senior official of one of the international regulatory bodies' who, in 'looking over the hundreds of pages of the brand new, highly quantitative, bank regulatory regime [Basel II]', said with a sigh: 'It does read a bit as if it has been written without adult supervision' (ibid.: xxiii). Such comments by those who write the rule books would seem to make external criticism superfluous.

Rules and effects

Finally, we can evaluate capital adequacy regulation in terms of the rules themselves and the effects they have. Perhaps the most important feature of the Basel system is that it offers financial institutions two alternative ways of determining their regulatory capital charges. The first is the so-called 'building block' approach, in which regulatory capital charges are set as minimum percentages of 'risk-weighted assets'. This process runs as follows:

- Assets are classed in terms of a limited number of risk categories.
- Each such category is given an arbitrary risk weight, which varies between 0 per cent (for example, for OECD government debt) and 100 per cent (for example, for equities).
- The risk-weighted assets are then obtained as the sum of the bank's assets each multiplied by its relevant risk weight.

One fairly obvious problem is that the risk weights are pulled out of thin air and bear little relationship to market reality. But a deeper problem is with the underlying principle that each asset can possibly have a fixed 'risk weight'. Elementary portfolio theory tells us that the risk of any asset in a portfolio – that is to say, its contribution to the risk of the portfolio – depends on the rest of the portfolio. The same asset might add a lot to the risk of one portfolio and yet subtract risk from another. The notion that an asset has a fixed 'risk weight' is therefore nonsense, but this nonsense is the very foundation on which the building block approach is built.

And what effect does this approach have? In a presentation to a conference on the financial crisis hosted by the Bruno Leoni Institute in Rome in early December 2008, Federico Foglia showed that almost all the leading financial institutions of the world have capital positions that are between one and two times their Basel minimum regulatory requirements. And yet these regulatory-compliant capital levels did not prevent many banks taking unsustainable risks. As he notes, 'Under

Basel II's most conservative [!] method, banks are, for instance, allowed a maximum of 10 times leverage in equity or 50 times AAA bonds', both of which represent 'amazing' and indeed 'unsustainable' levels of risk (Foglia, 2008). The riskiness of their positions is of course confirmed by the fact that many of these same institutions have defaulted or sought state aid over the last year. Thus, the capital adequacy regulatory systems have failed along with many of the banks they are meant to protect.

This takes us to the second approach offered by the Basel system. This approach allows banks to have their capital requirements determined by their own risk models. At first sight, this is much better and is at least consistent with basic portfolio theory. Unfortunately, this alternative approach has problems of its own:

- *The Risk Measure*: The approach is based on a risk measure, the value at risk (VaR), that is seriously inadequate and has been discredited for a long time. The main problem with the VaR is that it tells us how much we stand to lose on the worst of the good days – for example, on the worst of the best 99 days out of 100 hundred – but it gives us *no idea* what to expect on the one remaining day that really matters to us: the VaR is blind to 'tail risks', but it is the tail risks that we should be most concerned about (see Artzner et al., 1999; Dowd, 2005).
- *Gaming*: Traders have an incentive to 'game' the risk management system. They respond intelligently to the system, and identify and exploit its weaknesses (e.g. risks that are underestimated by the highly quantitative, data-driven models). The result is that the real risks being taken by an institution are likely to be greater than the firm's risk measurement system suggests, if only because no system is perfect and there are limits to the extent to which any system can take account of how those managed by it will react to it.
- *Systemic endogenous risk*: This occurs where individuals react to their environment and the environment reacts to them in a positive feedback loop that magnifies their losses. For example, when asset

prices fall and traders approach their position limits, then they will be forced to sell; this selling puts further downward pressure on asset prices, which then triggers more selling, and so on. Mitigating this problem requires institutions to have heterogeneous trading and risk management strategies, but the Basel system instead pressures them to react to shocks in similar ways (e.g. it pressures them to sell when a shock pushes VaR numbers up; see, for example, Danielsson and Shin, 2002).

- *Procyclicality*: Risks vary procyclically over the business cycle. This means that as the cycle approaches its peak risk assessments will fall, leading risk-based capital requirements to fall and lending to rise just at the point where the danger of a systemic downturn is greatest. As a consequence, risk-based capital regulation (such as Basel II) not only makes crises more likely but also makes them more severe as well (Danielsson et al., 2001).

It can also be added that the data-driven models used in VaR analysis discourage management from taking a conceptual view of the risks an institution is taking. Certain risks might build up and compound each other but the nature of the past behaviour of the assets that give rise to those risks is such that these risks are not reflected in the statistical models that banks are encouraged to use by the Basel II capital-setting process. The models first of all hide the underlying risks but, also, the encouragement to use quantitative models gives management false comfort that the risks of complex balance sheets, which are beyond anybody's understanding, can be modelled in a precise way. Management and shareholders therefore become more comfortable than they otherwise would with complex financial exposures. While it could be argued that banks should use approaches to risk management supplementary to those required by regulation, it is difficult in practice to avoid following the routes indicated as desirable by regulators.

A solution to the VaR problem is presumably to replace the VaR with a better measure of risk, and there are many better risk measures available (e.g. the Expected Shortfall, which is the loss that can be expected on that one bad day out of 100). Unfortunately, the other problems are much more intractable and suggest that the Basel approach to capital regulation is unsound even in principle.

There is, thus, yet another delightful paradox at the heart of the Basel system. The first Basel measurement approach, the building block approach, is unsound because it does not take account of modern risk theory, and the second is unsound because it does.

Conclusions

Capital adequacy regulation – and the Basel regime in particular – has failed dismally to protect the institutions it was meant to help: if the collapse of the financial system represents the 'success' of the Basel regime, then it is difficult to imagine what 'failure' might look like. To the extent that it had any impact at all, capital adequacy regulation would seem to have been seriously counterproductive – it appears to have saddled financial institutions with a large and useless compliance burden, hampered the development of best practice in risk management, undermined market competition and destabilised the world financial system. Its effectiveness is also undermined by the scope it creates for regulatory arbitrage and 'gaming' to circumvent its rules. These are the effects we should have expected all along, however: after all, capital adequacy regulation never had a strong rationale in the first place, and the group-think process that produces it is, to say the least, highly unlikely to come up with a rule book that makes any coherent sense. Proposals to patch Basel up, improve regulation and so on are essentially siren calls: Basel is bust beyond repair. If we wish to rebuild the world financial system, we need to go back and study the unregulated financial systems of an earlier and more stable age.

References

Artzner, P., F. Delbaen, J.-M. Eber and D. Heath (1999), 'Coherent measures of risk', *Mathematical Finance*, 9(3): 203–28.

Benston, G. J. and G. G. Kaufman (1986), 'The appropriate role of banking regulation', *Economic Journal*, 106(436): 688–97.

Danielsson, J. and H. S. Shin (2002), 'Endogenous risk', Mimeo, Financial Markets Group, London School of Economics.

Danielsson, J., P. Embrechts, C. Goodhart, C. Keating, F. Muennich, O. Renault and H. S. Shin (2001), 'An academic response to Basel II', London School of Economics Financial Markets Group Special Paper no. 130.

Dowd, K. (1999), 'Does asymmetric information justify bank capital adequacy regulation?', *Cato Journal*, 19(1): 39–41.

Dowd, K. (2005), *Measuring Market Risk*, 2nd edn, Chichester: John Wiley.

Foglia, F. (2008), Presentation to the Istituto Bruno Leoni conference 'The Challenge of Financial Instability for Market Capitalism', Rome, December.

Kaufman, G. G. (1987), 'The truth about bank runs', Staff Memorandum 87–3, Federal Reserve Bank of Chicago.

Miles, D. (1995), 'Optimal regulation of deposit taking financial intermediaries', *European Economic Review*, 39: 1365–84.

Rebonato, R. (2007), *Plight of the Fortune Tellers*, Princeton, NJ: Princeton University Press.

7 REGULATORY ARBITRAGE AND OVER-REGULATION

James Alexander[1]

I believe that banking institutions are more dangerous to our liberties than standing armies. If the American people ever allow private banks to control the issue of their currency, first by inflation, then by deflation, the banks and corporations that will grow up around [the banks] will deprive the people of all property until their children wake-up homeless on the continent their fathers conquered. The issuing power should be taken from the banks and restored to the people, to whom it properly belongs.

ATTRIBUTED TO THOMAS JEFFERSON, FIRST PRESIDENT
OF THE UNITED STATES (1743–1826)

Jefferson was right to be sceptical of banks, but was he right to think that the 'people' would be any better at running the money supply than private banks? Or that the 'people' could regulate the banks? What would he have said about the 'Too Big to Fail' principle now 100 per cent enshrined in practice, if not law?

The epic scale of the banking crisis easily justifies some very radical thinking on the regulation of banking. It is not good enough to propose mere tinkering with the regulatory system. The truly enormous supervisory, licensing and regulatory structures surrounding banks and financial services have failed to ensure sound and prudent banks. In fact, I would argue that these state structures have made the situation far worse. Banks have become so much part of the state corporatist world that 'private' ownership is only nominal. The banks are largely out of anyone's control. They are so large and powerful they are able to do

---

1   The views expressed in this chapter are the personal opinions of the author and do not represent those of M&G Investment Management.

more or less as they please – even though everything they do is regulated. Perhaps regulation is the problem rather than the solution.

The credit cycle

In the most dangerous stage of a credit bubble, it becomes widely believed that a new paradigm or stage of development has been entered whereby credit cycles are things of the past. This scenario is preventable. As Paul Volker once said, the job of a central bank is to take away the punchbowl just as the party is getting started. The credit cycle needs the oxygen of money and credit creation to keep going. Why wasn't the recent bubble spotted and prevented, given so much accumulated knowledge of past cycles? I would argue that improvements in bank regulation were a sham, cementing a belief that banks were improving risk controls, while bankers were really thinking of cleverer ways to circumvent the rules.

The banks and credit

The credit cycle can be stoked by loose central bank monetary policy and also via banks themselves depositing with each other and lending to each other. In a free market one would expect some banks to be 100 per cent reserve banks and others fractional reserve banks. Higher returns on deposits would be possible at the fractional reserve banks because they can recycle deposits as loans or other risky investments – and thus pay depositors more interest. Banks with higher reserves would be safer but pay less interest, or even none at all if holding, for instance, 100 per cent cash or gold reserves. There are problems, probably inflationary ones, involved with the transition from 100 per cent reserve banking to fractional reserve banking, but once that transition is made the question arises as to what is the prudent level of fractional reserve – 10 per cent, 20 per cent, 30 per cent? The ratio fell out of fashion over the last fifty years or so as the maintenance of such reserves was perceived to be a tax on banks as the reserves were typically held in unremunerated or lowly remunerated accounts with the central bank. As banks internationalised, those with tough local regulators who required high ratios were put at a disadvantage to those with softer regimes. Such required reserve ratios have been superseded for prudential regulatory purposes by the capital-to-assets ratio. This switch actually represented a pretty fundamental shift in the way banks are viewed – and a disastrous one, as it has turned out.

Reserve ratios morph into capital ratios as depositors lose their primacy

The focus on depositors is relegated in its importance within a structure that focuses on capital and not reserves, and that on shareholders is raised. Regulators have gradually moved their focus on to whether a bank has enough capital given its assets to prevent it from failing. It simply became assumed that there would be enough liquid assets to cover any unusual demands from depositors for their cash.

How much capital is required became the question, rather than what fractional reserve was appropriate. 'Reserves' used to mean cash held with the central bank and very short-term government securities, and their level was as high as 20 to 30 per cent half a century ago, but over time this ratio has fallen to almost nothing.

Banks now struggle to avoid the effects of capital regulations or, worse, shape the regulations to suit themselves. So much of the former activity, known as 'regulatory arbitrage' in the trade, goes on that it becomes one of the main goals of the banks and the key to making apparently high returns on capital.

Every regulated firm knows that getting on well with the regulators is key to controlling its destiny. As the economics of regulation, and everyday observation, make clear, capturing the regulators becomes an unconscious (and sometimes conscious) goal. And it is a goal that most regulated companies usually achieve. The end result is effective self-regulation, but with the appearance of real independent regulation.

Self-regulation with the appearance of regulation is misselling by the companies and by the state that allows it to happen, as it leads to consumers and other counterparties trusting regulated companies because of the official stamp of regulation.

More regulation as the regulators respond to failure of regulation

Modern banking capital regulation is an international phenomenon. It grew out of the ashes of the 1970s LDC debt crisis which nearly bankrupted a generation of banks. Into the partial void had stepped the Japanese banks. The Japanese 'economic miracle' is well known, but less well known is the role of their banks in recycling the trade surpluses that flowed into their banks as deposits. These deposits fuelled a massive expansion of the Japanese banks' balance sheets, and the banks went on a lending and spending spree both in Japan and the rest of the world. These banks paid little attention to leverage, however, and more experienced overseas bankers and their regulators spotted this flaw. Japanese regulators seemed happy to endorse the dash for global leadership by their banks. Other bankers and regulators, however, were a little more alert.

The banks and many of their regulators argued that it was not enough merely to rely on unsophisticated capital/assets ratios, as 'capital' meant different things in different countries. In the USA capital usually meant shareholders' equity; in other countries it could mean merely a guarantee from a government to absorb losses. Capital could also refer to the debt capital of a bank. Assets were also recognised as having a huge variability in riskiness, so simple regulation by a capital/assets ratio was correctly recognised as being a very blunt instrument.

As a first step international banks and their regulators, through the Basel-based Bank for International Settlements, agreed on standard minimum capital-to-assets ratios, but with a fairly simple set of definitions for capital and 'risk-weighting' of assets. Under Basel I, as it came to be known, capital was classified into high-quality, primary loss-absorbing Equity Capital (Tier One or 'Core' Capital) and Other Capital (or Tier Two Capital) such as subordinated debt capital. The two sorts of capital added together made up 'Total Capital'.

Assets were classified according to their risk. The market was already effectively pricing the assets for their risk, as reflected by the margins or spreads over risk-free assets they earned. The bankers and regulators were concerned that some banks, in particular Japanese ones, were not accurately pricing for the risks, undercutting Western banks in the process. Forcing all international banks to allocate the same capital to particular assets should in theory have resulted in more appropriate pricing, assuming all banks targeted the same returns on capital. On reflection, Basel I could also be seen as a form of economic protectionism against upstart new entrants – as well as having a more well-intentioned aim of encouraging prudence among internationally operating banks.

In the weighting system, corporate debt was 100 per cent risk-weighted, mortgages 50 per cent, loans to OECD banks 20 per cent and loans to OECD governments 0 per cent. The minimum Tier One Capital to Risk-Weighted Assets was set at 4 per cent and the Total Capital to Risk-Weighted Assets minimum at 8 per cent. The 'market' pretty quickly decided that 6 per cent and 10 per cent were more realistic minimums.

Basel I: good in theory, weak in practice

From the start, however, this attempt at a sort of world government regulation for banks was beset with problems. All sorts of special definitions or exemptions were allowed for Tier One and Tier Two Capital. For example:

- The Japanese and others were allowed to count unrealised gains on their extensive holdings of equities as Tier One capital.
- Other countries allowed their banks to include unrealised gains on real estate, a highly illiquid asset.
- Yet other banks were allowed to count various 'non-dilutive', fixed-

coupon-paying debt capital instruments in their core capital; such securities were definitely not Tier One primary loss-absorbing instruments, but could be called into action only once equity had been wiped out.

- Various German banks were allowed to include informal guarantees of support from local or federal government owners.
- US banks were almost all excluded since hardly any operated internationally, and the local regulators preferred to go it alone.
- Internationally operating US investment banks were also excluded as they were not really banks in the sense of deposit collectors, but 'broker-dealers' and thus regulated by the SEC.

Weak implementation and long transition periods meant the new rules came too late to save the Japanese banks. When the Japanese asset bubble burst and their stock market crashed their banks' 'capital' crashed too and the losses on their property loans and other assets swamped their tiny, underlying equity capital, resulting in effective insolvency and state- (taxpayer-) backed rescues.

Back to the bubble

The 1990s were a good decade for banks, as not only did interest rates fall following the defeat of inflation, but the collapse of the USSR and the embracing of economic liberalism in the former communist bloc and in China led to a peace dividend and a massive expansion in world trade. It was a golden age in retrospect.

Banks became more confident once again: the blip of the Asian crisis, the Russian default and the LTCM collapse were handled rather smoothly. The bursting of the Internet bubble and related corporate scandals such as Enron were similarly taken in their stride, though in retrospect it is clear that this was partly because the US central bank in particular held interest rates too low for too long.

But, just as the price of liberty is eternal vigilance, so the price of banking stability is eternal prudence. Prudence was neither fashionable nor helpful in keeping up return on capital at the banks. The spirit of the age was deregulation in all things, including banking. But deregulation in banking was really changed regulation, and a move away from prudence. Everyone agreed that oversight by the government was the ultimate guarantee of banks' solvency – thus rendering prudence apparently unnecessary. But was the government aware of the changes for which it was becoming responsible?

Deregulation or abrogation?

The old separation between banks and brokers (specifically between deposit collectors and securities firms) in the USA was abolished as the Glass-Steagall Act was repealed. The separation between JP Morgan and Morgan Stanley was no more. JP Morgan could compete to originate and sell securities, and Morgan Stanley could become a bank, collecting funding and making loans. The separation had been put in place because of fears that the Great Crash had been partly caused by banks that collected deposits engaging in securities trading. In the late 1920s, securities held by banks fell in value, wiping out depositors.

The upshot of the repeal was that broker-dealers became 'banks', or at least 'investment banks' – with large and diverse balance sheets. The investment banks weren't considered quite safe enough to be allowed to collect deposits from retail customers, but could access wholesale finance markets for their funding, i.e. deposits, but at arm's length from depositors. The securities firms' stated balance sheets went from around 20 per cent of US GDP to at least 100 per cent in the eight years following the Act's repeal in 1999. The spirit of US deregulation encouraged the European banks in particular to embark on a great expansion in the wholesale and investment banking activities of their commercial banks.

Basel I avoided

Banks became theoretically more sophisticated as they became bigger. Risk was supposedly measured more scientifically using statistical modelling of loss expectations. Feeding in data from previous market episodes allowed a greater confidence in the ability to predict the risk of engaging in a particular activity. Basel I was increasingly seen as simplistic, in particular with regard to its risk-weightings of assets. For example, a loan to a large blue-chip company was statistically far less risky than a loan to a small hotelier, but they had the same risk weightings.

The straitjacket of Basel I was leading to a great disintermediation of banks, whereby apparently wrongly risk-weighted assets[2] were being sold as securities to investors, bypassing the banks and leaving more risky, higher-margin assets on bank balance sheets. Although securitisation had been around for a long time prior to Basel I, it received a huge boost. It was regarded by many as a good thing because it dispersed risk around the market.

Some would argue that this was all a process of markets working more efficiently, as the simplistic Basel I regulations and resulting distortions were simply arbitraged away and investors' capital could continue to flow to its most rewarding uses. If banks couldn't make money on the assets because the regulatory capital charges were too high then the market would find a solution.

On the other hand, it could be argued that the Basel I rules were there for a purpose, a prudential purpose designed to prevent a reckless expansion of credit. If this is the case then regulatory arbitrage was not only unethical but dangerous. The apologists for regulatory arbitrage might have had a case if banks had not gone out of their way to hyperactively participate in the origination and structuring of these securities. In many cases also, banks actively financed buyers of these securities, often hedge funds. In other cases they created the Special Purpose Vehicles

---

2   Assets that were not particularly risky but which demanded high risk weightings.

(SIVs, Conduits, CLOs, etc.) that bought the securities and then offered 'liquidity' guarantees to these vehicles that ended up as guarantees of value too. Thus, the risks might well stay with the banks, and are now ending up back on the banks' balance sheets too. Unfortunately the banks cannot afford this risk and they are now being transferred to the taxpayers, in the UK via the government's Asset Protection Scheme.

The buyers of these securities were financed with, for example, rolling 364-day loans rather than higher capital-charged one-year-and-above loans. The new financing, or the 'liquidity' guarantees, then had lower risk weightings than the loans the bank was offloading.

The constant repackaging of risky loans into less risky securities also aided this process.

The corruption of the ratings agencies

A great new business line sprang up for the credit-rating agencies, which had previously merely judged the creditworthiness of a few hundred institutions such as governments, major banks and large companies. They could now pass judgement on hundreds of thousands of individual securities and their various tranches.

This would have been a good thing if the buyers of the securities had been paying for the ratings. The agencies, though, came to be hired by and captured by the originators and structurers of the securities, and the ratings were little more than a very sophisticated form of advertising. The very obvious conflict of interest was corrupting. At the peak of the securitisation mania over 80 per cent of ratings agency fees came from structured credit work paid for by the banks.

The agencies were supposed to be guardians of the risk categorisation models, and could then be paid to ensure that certain packages met the requirements of the models. This whole process was sanctified by the regulators, who gave the ratings agencies their blessing as Nationally Recognised Securities Rating Organisations (NRSROs) and increasingly relied on them as the official arbiters of risk.

Regulators made things worse by embedding these ratings in the modern risk-weightings regime brought in over several years, codified in Basel II. In its basic form, or Foundation Approach, Basel II used external credit ratings to decide on the risk weighting of assets. But the corruption of the ratings agencies meant that risk weightings could and should not be relied upon. In its more sophisticated form Basel II allowed banks to dispense with ratings agencies; they could use their own risk-based modelling – if the individual national regulator approved the system.

Effectively, the banks were becoming their own regulators – though they all had to use a similar approach to regulation. There was no market in regulation and there was no way contracting parties could choose between banks regulated in different ways. The banks had simply captured government regulation.

In an otherwise good speech, Andrew Haldane, Executive Director for Financial Stability at the Bank of England ('Why banks failed the stress test', 13 February 2009), seemed to want to pin the blame for failed regulation on 'market failure' when all players in the market were implicitly (and often explicitly) operating under the assumption that government would bail out banks if the models failed, as Haldane makes very clear. Who was right, the market or the regulators? I guess that Haldane, like all regulators, couldn't see the real cause, and probably the real solution. Regulatory failure should result in the abolition of regulation, but then turkeys don't vote for Christmas.

Basel II leads to disaster

The upshot from the transition towards the introduction of Basel II was a final, dramatic increase in leverage at the banks as the modelled risk of their assets went ever lower, and their notional balance sheets ever higher. Many banks argued that they were becoming less risky, less leveraged owing to the sophistication of the modelling allowing better gauges of risk. Although the regulators decreed no less capital would be in the system under Basel II versus Basel I, banks rushed to put that newly freed-up capital to work. Pro forma Basel II capital ratios were often one or two percentage points lower than under Basel I, and some banks mooted hugely generous capital returns. As the regulators said no, banks added more 'low-risk' assets to their balance sheets and the last hurrah of the bubble ensued.

Finance directors and chief executives were often bewildered by questions on the size of the balance sheet or the old-fashioned capital/ assets ratio. They would say they never looked at the balance sheet, only the results of their risk modelling. It was a madness ultimately driven by the application of mistaken statistical techniques to real economy players and activities underpinned by regulatory approval.

Real people behave more or less rationally; they take out mortgages and pay them back. If the mortgage customers do this well for a long period, the risk of lending to them does fall. The pattern of behaviour is thus rewarded by lower prices as new capital is attracted to arbitrage away the excess profit earned by the first-mover mortgage loan providers. In the modern financial system capital may begin to flood the market rather quickly; demand for loans to package up begins to drive the market rather than any customers' ability to repay. The subtle but incremental changes in the market are not captured by the statistical modelling. The poor original modelling has in fact allowed the bubble to be created, unintentionally of course, but effectively bringing into being the monster that ultimately consumes the models.

It would be better to move back to unregulated banking with 'buyer beware' as the guiding rule rather than the artificial confidence that is derived from state regulation and the 'too big to fail' guarantee of a state (and taxpayer) bailout when all else fails.

It gets worse

The two forms of regulatory arbitrage outlined above, the transfer of loans to less heavily capital-charged entities and the repackaging of risky loans, were the most common. Another area of regulatory arbitrage was artificial 'insurance' bought from specialist structured credit 'insurers'. Again, like the risk transfer of the regulatory arbitrage described above, credit insurance does have innocent and seemingly well-intentioned beginnings.

The fundamental mistake of using, or abusing, statistics in economics appeared again here. In normal insurance claims risks aren't usually correlated. Fires don't sweep across whole regions and car crime remains isolated and predictable. Hurricanes hardly ever happen, but are a well-known and modelled catastrophe risk. Economic risks are correlated, however, and can even be self-fulfilling, especially at times of boom or bust. As a result, credit insurers cannot hope to survive a bad recession, but are a very useful way for banks to lower risk weightings of assets in a boom and hence lower capital charges, and thus raise returns on capital on a given set of assets. AIG was particularly helpful here, especially as it was an insurance company not regulated as a bank and, just to be on the safe side, it operated its credit insurance through a completely unregulated subsidiary. Of course this unit had the very best credit rating money could buy.

Credit default swaps (CDS) bulked together into synthetic collateralised debt obligations (CDOs) were presented as performing a similarly innocent function of spreading credit risk through the financial system (not just by the banks but by regulators and central banks too). But they have similar defects to sub-prime and other mortgage securitisations. In fact CDS prospered more as a way of arbitraging ratings agency ratings, a subset of regulatory arbitrage.

Structurers created vehicles that were composed of well-rated but poorly priced synthetic corporate debt (the CDS), a form of credit insurance. The CDS were then packaged together at 100 a time to create the specialist, capital-light instruments (synthetic CDOs). Protection for the investor in the CDO came from using the correlation tables of the rating agencies and others that 'proved' the individual corporate borrowers on whom these credit insurance contracts (or CDS) were written would not have highly correlated defaults, thus limiting the probability of huge payouts if defaults all came at the same time. The gross written volume of single-name corporate CDS, and closely related indices of CDS, reached $60 trillion by the end of 2007. We are not reassured by the main banks involved claiming that the netting of this amount down to a few trillion means we should not be too concerned by this market.

Sadly, the benign assumption of no correlation proved optimistic. Worse was that most of the 'wrongly priced' corporate CDS packaged in the CDOs, according to the ratings agencies but not the market, were on financial companies. These CDOs would often include the very financial companies (investment banking arms of large universal banks, investment banks, insurers, specialist credit insurers) that were writing the CDS that provided the credit insurance. This was a hugely damaging circularity akin to the old Lloyds insurance spiral. In particular, the specialist credit insurers came to be seen as almost pure creations of the credit rating agencies. Actual downgrades and defaults at credit insurers would leave swathes of the structured credit market in tatters and trigger huge losses amongst investors.

Regulatory arbitrage took many more sophisticated forms. The rocket scientists working in the financial sector that you hear about were often focused on trying to run rings around regulators, ratings agencies and auditors – but were more often working hand in hand with these groups, as all were using the same flawed risk-modelling techniques.

Back to the future

Banking by this time had moved very far from its roots as a store of value and facilitator of exchange. Provision of capital, the old preserve of the UK's merchant banks, had become the overriding priority. Of course, there were always highly prudent banks and building societies that had very carefully lent out deposits to those customers they knew well, either mortgage customers or companies, but it was very tightly controlled as protection of deposits was the most important goal.

We need to go back to this world. Banks need to be trusted. They do not need to do anything too complex, especially based on a misuse of statistics and a misunderstanding of economic relationships: leave that to the pure financial speculators, and let them fail when they go wrong. 'Narrow banking', as some call it, needs to make a comeback – despite the patronising ridicule of Adair Turner, who described it as a return to the days of 'Captain Mainwaring'.[3]

But even with narrow banks, there needs to be the fear of failure to keep them honest, failure that will cost equity owners all their capital and even threaten unsecured creditors if necessary. There needs to be many of them too, and they should not be too big – the notion of a financial institution as 'too big to fail' must be seen as false. This will not come about by regulatory design but by market choice – if decision-makers are allowed to take responsibility for their decisions. The eagerness to regulate financial institutions and ever perfect and refine that regulation has, in fact, led to the precise opposite of the intended effects, a massively false sense of reassurance.

If there are to be regulators it should be made very clear that they are not there to provide guarantees, they will be prone to capture by those they regulate and that no banks are too big to fail. Of course, if all this were made clear then there would be little point to their existence. So perhaps we should make do without them and accept that we will always live in an imperfect world and should act prudently as a result.

---

3   See *The Economist*'s inaugural City Lecture given by Adair Turner on 21 January 2009, www.fsa.gov.uk/pages/Library/Communication/Speeches/2009/0121_at.shtml.

8 BANKING REGULATION AND THE LENDER-OF-LAST-RESORT ROLE OF THE CENTRAL BANK
Tim Congdon

Banks are strange institutions. They can epitomise the free market at its best and also indulge in some of the worst forms of financial skulduggery just on the right side of the law; they are both the standard-bearers of the capitalist system and, too often, its worst advertisement.

But for the layperson perhaps the oddest feature of banking is its mathematics. When non-bank businesses deal with each other they assume, correctly in most cases, that the assets – the land, the buildings, the machinery – belong largely or wholly to their shareholders. But banking is not like that at all. Instead most banks' assets consist of loans and are owned to only a small extent by their shareholders. In a typical modern economy the part of the banks' assets that belong to shareholders – the capital – is typically less than 5 per cent of the total. In the jargon, banks' capital-to-asset ratios are under 5 per cent. The capital is needed to protect the banks' depositors (who own over 95 per cent of the claims on a bank) against bad risks in the loan portfolios.

When this is explained to most people, their first reaction is to run. However, British high-street banks have operated with capital-to-asset ratios of about 5 per cent for many decades and their customers have been able safely to deposit money and withdraw it on literally billions of occasions. The point is that banks have learned how to ensure that their borrowing customers pay back loans in full and on time. In most years loan loss ratios are under 0.75 per cent of assets and are comfortably exceeded by profits from interest income and an assortment of fees. But, every now and again, the banks take too many risks and the arithmetic turns sour.

In the years leading up to mid-2007 commercial banks – the UK's high-street banks and the USA's 'main-street' banks, the banks that take deposits from the public and process cheque payments – have purchased large quantities of so-called 'structured finance products' from investment banks.[1] (Investment banks differ from commercial banks in two main respects, that they trade and underwrite securities instead of making loans, and that they operate on even lower capital-to-asset ratios.) The typical 'structured finance product' bought by a high-street/main-street bank has in principle been very safe and at issue was given a triple-A rating by the credit rating agencies. These triple-A securities ought to repay 100 cents in the dollar, 100 pence in the pound, 100 cents in the euro and so on. The great majority of them probably will repay in this way, despite the recent shenanigans.

Unfortunately in mid-2007 the wholesale money markets, through which banks borrow from and lend to each other, closed up. This happened for a wide variety of reasons, of which the most important was the fall in US house prices and the implications of that fall for the value of the structured finance securities. Triple-A securities dropped in value, often by 10 to 20 per cent. So if such securities were, say, 10 per cent of high-street bank assets, they had lost 1 or 2 per cent of the value of all their assets. That sounds trifling; hardly enough to threaten the banks' charitable donations let alone the future of capitalism. But here comes the vicious arithmetic. A drop in the value of total assets of 2 per cent[2] wipes out 40 per cent of the capital of an organisation, such as a bank, whose assets are represented by share capital only to the extent of 5 per cent. According to a strict interpretation of rules that have been developed by international financial bureaucrats in Basel over the last twenty years, a bank that has lost a big chunk of its capital must shrink its assets to restore the sacred capital-to-assets ratio to its original level.

---

1   These are securities, often complex, that can be bought and sold in financial markets. The capital and interest payments from the securities are often determined by the capital and interest payments received from an underlying set of loans made by a bank which is sometimes known as the 'originator'.

2   Caused by a drop in the value of particular assets of 20 per cent.

If losses are widespread, across a number of banks, a ghastly downward spiral, known as 'debt deflation', can now engulf the system. The banks can shrink their assets by selling off securities or forcing their customers to repay loans. But these sales of securities aggravate the fall in their price. Forcing customers to repay loans is even more gruesome. As loan portfolios decline, so also does the level of bank deposits. Bank deposits are the principal form of money in today's world. If the quantity of money goes down, so do asset prices, incomes and spending.

None of the above – despite its overwhelming significance for employment and living standards – is rocket science. Ben Bernanke, the chairman of the Federal Reserve, has written extensively about the Great Depression of the 1930s, the worst example so far of a downward debt-deflation spiral. The final research paper published in 1993 by Mervyn King for the London School of Economics' Financial Markets Group, and probably prepared just before his move to the Bank of England as chief economist, was on debt deflation.

The downward spiral is caused by a logjam that prevents market agents from pricing assets correctly. The textbook answer is well known and was applied by the Bank of England on many occasions in the nineteenth and twentieth centuries. To say that the central bank, perhaps assisted by the government, must move into the markets and buy up every decent security in sight would be a simplification, but it would not be caricature. Instead of the triple-A securities trading at 80 or 85 cents, heavy official purchases could raise the price to 90 or 95 cents. The banks could start to write back their capital and to lend again, bringing the crisis to an end.

Key American economists and officials knew in late 2008 that big government or central bank purchases of securities had to be one item on the policy agenda in an extreme crisis of the kind they then faced. That was the original rationale for the Paulson plan ('the Troubled Assets Relief Program') of a fund of up to $700 billion to buy in the blighted securities held by the banks. It was a sensible thing to do, but Congress didn't like Paulson's chumminess with the bankers, particularly the possibility that the troubled assets would be bought at too high a price.

In the end much of the $700 billion was used for a related, but different, purpose. With a lack of capital in the banking system identified as the central problem, US policymakers decided to invest a few hundred billion dollars in bank equity. Following a precedent set by the Reconstruction Finance Corporation in the 1930s, banks issued preference stock to the government at a moderate rate of interest well beneath their expected return on capital. This was not altogether a soft option for the bankers, however, since the issues of preference stock usually had an attachment of warrants to ordinary equity. If the warrants are exercised a few years from now when banks' share prices have recovered, the result could be a large capital gain for the government and a dilution of the original shareholders' stake.

Indeed, a larger question raised by the global financial emergency of late 2008 was the relative merits of different approaches to banks' problems. Traditional central bank action consisted of a combination of asset purchases to boost cash in the banking system and lender-of-last-resort assistance to institutions in particular difficulty, and implied no direct threat to bank shareholders' rights. (Last-resort loans might have to be at penalty rates and so reduce banks' profits, but they were still loans to be repaid, not new equity.) The new feature of the latest crisis, capital injections from the state, may appear to deal directly with the lack of banking system capital, but the government – with its immense regulatory and fiscal powers – has been able to dictate terms and override shareholder rights. Arguably, a significant threat to private property rights has emerged.

Particularly in the British case, the terms of the October 2008 recapitalisation exercise seem to have been oppressive. The Financial Services Authority and the Bank of England concocted a planning scenario in which a severe recession led to heavy loan losses and eroded banks' capital, and then they and the government required the banks to raise over £35 billion of capital ahead of the event. If banks do not have heavy loan losses in 2010, 2011 and subsequently, they will have an unnecessarily large amount of capital, much of which they did not seek. While existing shareholders were given the option to subscribe the new equity, many investors had been traumatised by the British government's cavalier attitude towards shareholder rights in the recent nationalisations of Northern Rock and Bradford & Bingley. They were understandably nervous about possible future expropriation of their assets.[3]

HSBC, which could be viewed as a Hong Kong Chinese bank, spurned the government's initiative, while Barclays raised extra capital from foreign investors in the Middle East. Nevertheless, the government acquired 60 per cent of the Royal Bank of Scotland at a price well beneath net asset value and could ultimately make a large profit on its holding. The profit would clearly be at the expense of the previous shareholders. Some commentators would regard such an outcome as fair and reasonable, since RBS had allegedly run its business in too adventurous a fashion. The loss to the previous shareholders would be galling, however, even outrageous, if the triple-A securities do in the end pay back at par.

RBS management might claim that their problem – like that of Northern Rock and Bradford & Bingley – arose from the largely unforeseeable breakdown of the international wholesale market in interbank lending. They might argue that the traditional response would have been a loan from the Bank of England (plus purchases of assets, such as the contentious triple-A securities, by the Bank), which would have given them time to rearrange their assets and would have left shareholders' equity unaffected. Whatever the validity of this view, it seems inescapable that future investors in the British banking industry will be worried about the safety of their property rights. Some capital will move

---

3   The author holds shares in both Northern Rock and Bradford & Bingley. He wrote an expert witness statement for the Northern Rock shareholders in the legal action against the government arising from the 2008 Banking (Special Provisions) Act. The claimants in this case (i.e. the Northern Rock shareholders) believe that the terms of the legislation undermine their property rights and are a breach of the 1998 Human Rights Act.

abroad to other centres, such as New York, Hong Kong and Singapore, along with skilled staff and support infrastructure. The long-term effects on Britain's financial services sector could be dire.

The banking crisis of 2007 and 2008 was multifaceted and complex. Blame for the problems in Britain, which was only one country caught up in the turmoil, has to be apportioned widely. The banking industry itself, the UK's own policymaking apparatus and the international regulatory machinery all made mistakes. Fundamental issues are raised about whether a central bank should restrict itself to economic research and the setting of interest rates, or should instead carry out its time-honoured role as 'the bankers' bank'.[4] Whereas the USA's Federal Reserve expanded its balance sheet dramatically in late 2008 to help the financial system and so the economy at large, the governor of the Bank of England, Mr Mervyn King, denied that a central bank could make long-term loans to private sector agents. His attitude seemed to be that, if British banks had trouble in financing their assets, this was a problem for them and the government, and not for the Bank of England. At any rate, the damage to the British banking industry – which had been one of the UK's few success stories in international competition – is likely to be severe and long-lasting.

---

4   The issues are discussed at greater length in the author's *Central Banking in a Free Society*, published by the Institute of Economic Affairs in March 2009.

9 ACCOUNTING ASPECTS OF THE FINANCIAL CRISIS

D. R. Myddelton

Introduction

The worldwide financial crisis in the autumn of 2008 had many causes, including reckless government monetary and fiscal policies and defective regulation. The requirement to use fair value ('mark-to-market') accounting may also have been partly to blame.

Some banks overstated their assets by failing to make proper provision for losses on so-called toxic securities. On the other hand, in assessing capital adequacy, some solvent banks – following the rules – marked certain financial instruments to market in abnormal, distressed conditions. In both cases the margins of error may have been enormous. There is also concern that users of accounts may not properly understand the implications of some off-balance-sheet assets and liabilities.

In recent years, new accounting standards have been brought in which require banks to use market values and market information in valuing assets and liabilities. Specifically, International Accounting Standards IAS 32 and IAS 39 deal with disclosure and measurement of financial instruments. These so-called 'fair value' rules also formed the basis for the Basel II capital requirements for banks. An assessment of a bank's assets and liabilities using information about their market value would determine whether they had sufficient capital to satisfy the regulators. In mid-October 2008 changes to allow more flexibility from 1 July 2008[1] brought International Financial Reporting Standards more into

---

1   The changes could have a retroactive effect.

line with US Generally Accepted Accounting Principles. But this was after the damage had been done.

One important lesson is that it is not much use people following the rules and ticking boxes if the rules themselves are ill judged. Another is that rivalry between standard-setting bodies can be healthy: in Hayek's famous words, 'competition is a discovery procedure'. All financial institutions were required to use the same procedure for reporting and thus, when the rules were found to be inappropriate, they affected many banks in a similar way at the same time.

Book value of assets

There are two ways that a business decides at what value to show assets in its accounts. A business that is a 'going concern' normally shows assets at cost. But on the rare occasions when a business is reckoned *not* to be a going concern, its balance sheet uses the 'liquidation' basis.

Even on a going-concern basis, accounts provide for unrealised losses in respect of *current* assets. Hence accounts show stocks and work-in-progress at an estimate of net realisable value where that is *lower* than cost; and trade debtors at the amounts due less any provision for expected bad debts.

Balance sheets normally show tangible fixed assets at cost less depreciation to date. The annual depreciation charges allocate the net cost over a fixed asset's life: they are not an attempt to 'revalue' the asset each year. In effect, they smooth the total lifetime write-off between periods. Accounts show intangible fixed assets at cost, less any impairment write-offs. These *do* represent a downward revaluation, though not on any regular basis. Valuing assets on a 'liquidation' basis assumes that *all* assets, both current and long-term, are to be sold immediately. This 'fire sale' approach, which can often involve drastic write-downs from cost, would be totally unrealistic for a going concern.

Marking to market

In the early 1990s, Enron was keen to use 'mark-to-market' accounting and managed to persuade its auditors, Arthur Andersen, that it should do so. Jeff Skilling (former chief executive of Enron) also convinced the US regulator, the Securities and Exchange Commission (SEC), that it should allow the company to use mark-to-market accounting. According to Eichenwald (2005) he argued: 'Accrual accounting lets you pretty much create the outcome you want, by keeping the bad stuff and selling the good. Mark-to-market does not let you do this.' Mark-to-market accounting requires a business to use the market value of its assets in its accounts, where the assets have an easily ascertainable market value. Clearly marketable and tradable securities do have such an easily ascertainable market value – at least in most conditions.

It is true that reporting only realised profits may tempt managers to *time* sales of certain assets to affect reported profits. But 'mark-to-market' accounting allows the inclusion of hypothetical 'profits' which may not be realised for many years into the future, if ever. The approach requires an active market with a large enough volume of independent trades. In severely distressed markets these conditions may not exist.

Alternative approaches to mark-to-market were generally preferred in the UK until recently. For example, in 1995 most members of the UK Accounting Standards Board preferred the 'actuarial' approach to valuing pension fund assets rather than the use of market values. The actuarial approach would involve an actuary making a judgement about the value of assets and liabilities, on a consistent basis, using information about market values but also using other information as deemed appropriate. The main reason for this preference was that market values were regarded as too volatile and as reflecting short-term fluctuations that were not a true reflection of the long-term cash flows that the assets would generate. But later the ASB (1998) agreed to move to market values 'in the interests of international harmonisation' – arguably a misguided compromise against its better judgement. IAS 39, which applied more broadly, later used a similar 'market value' approach.

Accounting for investments under IAS 39

The international accounting standard IAS 39 requires accounts to show 'financial assets at fair value through profit or loss' or 'available-for-sale financial assets'. Such is the normal procedure for many bank investments in financial instruments. 'Fair value' is the amount for which knowledgeable willing partners could exchange an asset or settle a liability in an arm's-length transaction. This definition assumes that such an amount is both known and reliable. In these circumstances the terms 'fair value' and 'market value' are interchangeable.

In contrast, balance sheets show investments at amortised cost if they are 'held-to-maturity investments' or 'loans or receivables'. 'Amortised cost' is broadly initial cost, minus repayments of principal, plus a proportion of any difference between initial cost and the amount due on maturity and less any impairment (for example, due to a reduction in creditworthiness of the borrower). This method is rather like providing for depreciation of tangible fixed assets. Assets carried at amortised cost still have to be written down to their recoverable value if impaired; but this involves estimating future cash flows and hence allows companies to take a longer-term, and possibly more optimistic, view rather than relying on current market values.

IAS 39 on Recognition and Measurement of Financial Instruments is not easy to interpret. Before the recent amendments it comprised 6 pages of Introduction; 32 pages (114 paragraphs) of Standard; 44 pages (138 paragraphs) of Application Guidance; 64 pages (227 paragraphs) of Basis of Conclusions; 5 pages of Dissenting Opinions and 121 pages of Illustrative Examples and Guidance. In all, 272 pages – the length of an average-sized book. Thus an apparently simple idea – marking to market – can be very complex to interpret in practice.

Problems in marking to market

The dangers of 'mark-to-market' accounting were highlighted recently on the German stock exchange (*Financial Times*, 28 October 2008). The state of Lower Saxony owned 20 per cent of the shares in Volkswagen, and Porsche owned 35 per cent. This left a 'free-float' proportion of 45 per cent of the shares freely traded on the exchange. But on 26 October Porsche revealed that, using derivatives, it had secretly increased its stake in Volkswagen to 74 per cent. This reduced the free float to just 6 per cent of the total outstanding shares. Many hedge funds, which had been selling Volkswagen's shares short, had to rush to cover their short positions after the announcement, with losses totalling some £10 billion.

As a result, in what had become a very illiquid market, hedge funds drove the marginal price of Volkswagen's shares up from €200 to more than €1,000 at one point. For a brief period, this apparently gave Volkswagen a higher nominal 'market capitalisation' than any other company in the world. But that derived from multiplying a spurious marginal price by *all* the shares in issue, even though 94 per cent of them were not available for trading. The prices of all the other 29 shares on the German DAX-30 Index fell that day; but the huge price rise in Volkswagen shares caused the index to *rise* by 1 per cent.

On a more modest scale, my father once bought some shares in a thinly traded listed South African gold mining company. He started buying at 17s 6d[2] and kept on buying until his last block of shares cost 45 shillings[3] each. He might then have 'valued' his entire holding at 45 shillings – by 'marking to market'. But in that case he would have been misleading himself. For had he tried to sell all his shares at once, he would probably have driven the price down again to roughly their starting level of 17s 6d.

What is the relevance of these particular incidents? They demonstrate directly one serious weakness in mark-to-market accounting and indirectly another weakness. Securities markets can become illiquid for a variety of reasons. If trading becomes thin, the price of shares and bonds can become very volatile and cease to reflect underlying value. Arguably this has happened in the markets in which banks have

---

2   87.5 pence.
3   £2.25.

operated and made losses – the markets for securitised debt. The opaque and specialised nature of these instruments, and the desire of banks to reduce their holdings of securities because of a shortage of capital, have led markets in securitised debt to become very illiquid. A vicious circle can be created. Illiquidity drives down the price; the value of banks' assets on a mark-to-market basis falls; banks become more unwilling to take on additional risks; they refuse to participate in the markets for securitised debt; the market becomes more illiquid; and so on.

Second, market values can be affected by herd-like behaviour of investors both when markets rise and when they fall. Bubbles can be created within securities markets. Mark-to-market accounting can lead investors to overestimate their capital in a bubble, which encourages them to take on more risks at the very time when the market might be about to turn. Similarly, if the market undershoots, when banks mark securities to current market values, then banks will appear to have less capital and may be reluctant to take on risks at a time when securities prices are at their lowest. Indeed, banks may try to contract their businesses at such a time. Both of these weaknesses in mark-to-market accounting may lead banks to appear insolvent in extreme cases.

Change in standards

Accounting standards determined the capital adequacy rules for banks under the Basel II Agreement. Thus the scenarios described above were not merely a theoretical possibility. In the recent illiquid markets banks had to write down the value of many financial instruments to distressed current 'market value'. Even though in the circumstances they might have chosen to hold them to maturity, the rules pertaining then did not allow banks to reclassify any of their financial instruments.

In mid-October 2008, under pressure from the European Union, the International Accounting Standards Board (IASB) amended IAS 39 to bring it more closely into line with the Financial Accounting Standard US FAS 115. This 'emergency' change did not go through the normal process of consultation. Companies are now permitted, as from 1 July 2008, to reclassify certain fair-value assets as 'held-to-maturity'. They can thus value them at amortised cost rather than marking to market. The retroactive nature of the change allows companies to cherry-pick which assets to treat in this way; though they must disclose how much difference it has made to the results.

For example, on 30 October 2008, by using the new accounting rules, Deutsche Bank recorded a profit instead of the expected loss (*Financial Times*, 31 October 2008). The bank reclassified nearly £20 billion of assets as loans that it will now hold until maturity – including £5 billion of funded leveraged finance loans (which it had intended should be sold on) and £8 billion in asset-backed commercial paper. Through this switch, Deutsche Bank, which announced £1 billion of write-downs, avoided further write-downs of £650 million. Arguably, however, this change came too late to save many banks. Such lack of speed and adaptability to a new situation is almost inevitable when all firms are required by internationally agreed regulations to use the same accounting standards, which can only be changed by regulators.

Marking to market versus economic value

The problems with marking to market described above are not just theoretical. There have been very serious manifestations of these problems during the current crisis – hence the eventual response by regulatory bodies. The markets for some assets held by banks were extremely thin owing to widespread lack of liquidity. Yet, prior to the recent amendment, the 'fair value' rules had required banks to write such assets down to the actual traded value of similar assets – even if they reflected quite atypical conditions and quantities. The illiquidity of markets during the crash and afterwards means that the apparent 'fair value' of an asset might be much less than the real economic value in the medium term.

For example, according to the Bank of England's October 2008 Financial Stability Report, because of defaults on underlying mortgages, credit losses on US sub-prime residential mortgage-backed securities (RMBS) could reach US$195 billion. Yet this was much less than the mark-to-market loss of US$310 billion. The difference stemmed from market participants demanding substantial discounts for uncertainty about the eventual scale of credit losses and illiquidity in the secondary market. Reflecting the risk of forced asset sales by distressed institutions, the current market values of AAA-rated UK prime RMBS also lay well below their economic values.

My conclusion is that if we had more freedom with regard to accounting practices there could be a sensible discussion among analysts, banks and others about how much bank assets are worth. Instead there has been a most unsatisfactory argument about how *regulators* wish to value banks' assets, which the evidence suggests may bear little relation to reality. As a result, perfectly solvent banks have had to write down some of their assets by huge amounts. This triggered all sorts of crisis arrangements to enable them to meet inappropriate capital adequacy requirements. Thus the economic consequences have been extremely serious.

References

ASB (Accounting Standards Board) (1998), 'Aspects of accounting for pension costs: discussion paper', London, pp. 8 and 11.

Eichenwald, K. (2005), *Conspiracy of Fools*, New York: Broadway Books, p. 59.

10 THE NON-PROBLEM OF SHORT SELLING
Laurence Copeland

In his 1985 Reith Lectures, David Henderson coined the expression DIY economics for the collection of commonsense propositions that every practical person knows to be true about economics: that exports are good, imports bad; that government spending creates jobs; that manufacturing is more important than service industry; that lower interest rates are always desirable; and so on. To this list of obvious but patently false notions, we need nowadays to add another: *that short sales are bad*.

If I expect Tesco shares to rise in value tomorrow, from say £2.00 to £2.50, I can buy them today in the hope of being able to sell them for a 25 per cent profit tomorrow. On the other hand, if I expect Tesco shares to fall in value, from £2.00 to £1.50, what should I do? Instead of a long position, I could go short – in other words, I could borrow 100 Tesco shares and sell them immediately at £2.00 each, bringing in £200. If I turn out to be right, I will be able to watch their price fall to £1.50, at which point I shall be able to buy them back again for £150, and return the borrowed shares to the lender, leaving me with a profit of 100 x £0.50 = £50. The key thing to note here is that going long and going short both involve speculation based on the trader's information. The long position, however, could make an unlimited profit if Tesco shares rise without limit, but stands to lose no more than £200 even if Tesco shares become worthless. By contrast, even if the share price falls to zero, the short position can gain no more than £200 but, on the other hand, stands to lose an unlimited amount if the price goes up, instead of down.

Both buying and selling transmit information to the market. In both cases, speculators are backing a belief that the stock in question is mispriced. Since there seems no reason to think that shares are always – or even most of the time – undervalued, there is no more justification for restricting short selling than for restricting buying.

Short selling is not the cause of falls in the prices of individual shares, let alone of the market as a whole. It is simply one of the ways in which the ultimate cause – the bad news – brings the price down. As far as shareholders are concerned, the clamour to ban shorting arises simply out of the urge to shoot the messenger bringing the bad tidings. As far as management is concerned, the motivation is straightforwardly self-serving.

The FSA surrendered to pressure to ban short selling of 29 (mainly financial) stocks for a limited period starting on 19 September 2008, in response to the near-collapse in the HBOS share price earlier in the week. The justification for the ban was, however, vague to say the least:

> While we still regard short-selling as a legitimate investment technique in normal market conditions, the current extreme circumstances have given rise to disorderly markets. As a result, we have taken this decisive action, after careful consideration, to protect the fundamental integrity and quality of markets and to guard against further instability in the financial sector. (FSA/ PN/102/2008, 18 September 2008)

Whether the market in HBOS shares was actually 'disorderly' (whatever that may mean) is unclear. First, on the day of the final collapse, only 2.75 per cent of HBOS shares were out on loan, compared with 18 per cent in July, when the HBOS rights issue started trading,[1] so it seems improbable that short sellers played a large part in any perceived problems. Second, even if short sellers had been out in force, the question might well be asked: why did they choose to short HBOS rather than any other bank – or indeed any other major stock? The sight of the predatory big cat pulling down the stragglers among a herd of

---

1 BBC, 19 September 2008, quoting research firm Data Explorers.

zebra may be unsettling, but it is nonetheless nature's way of preserving the health of the herd. HBOS was a lumbering beast wounded by excessive leverage and an asset portfolio dominated by mortgages secured on houses whose prices were already falling steeply.

Claims were made at the time that short sellers had been spreading damaging rumours about HBOS in order to drive down the price – 'short and distort', as the stratagem has sometimes been called. If there is any truth in this allegation, the problem is one of malicious rumour-mongering rather than short selling itself and can be dealt with under existing FSA regulations or criminal statutes. But even then, the question needs to be asked: why was this particular stock targeted? It should be remembered in any case that many rumours (e.g. about imminent take-overs) are positive for share prices and therefore generate substantial gains for long positions – yet nobody uses this as grounds for a ban on share purchases.

What would be the consequences of a permanent ban on short selling?

The first point to note is that, whether desirable or not, it is far from obvious that a ban would result in higher or less volatile share prices.[2] Investors might well be deterred from buying stocks if they knew that there may well already be bad news out in the market but not as yet reflected in the quoted price, leaving open the prospect of possible falls in the near future as owners of the stock progressively discover the truth and reduce their holdings. Moreover, those who took a pessimistic view could achieve the same result as a short sale by other means – for example, by the use of derivatives. Thus, if short sales were ruled out, an institution that expected the price to fall could buy a put option on the stock, though this possibility raises the question of whether put options would be available on any substantial scale, given that institutions must

---

2   Note that short selling has never been allowed in China, yet its stock market has fallen far more heavily than any other major market.

typically rely on short sales in order to hedge their exposure to the put options they write.

The last point raises the question of the wider implications of a ban for financial institutions. On the one hand, long-term investors such as pension funds rely on lending stock to short sellers so as to provide a modest boost to the return on the large portfolios they are forced to carry in the course of their normal business, so a ban would represent a loss to them.[3] On the other hand, medium-term investment institutions such as unit trusts have begun to offer structured products to the general public, which are essentially combinations of a long position in a stock portfolio (typically based on a major index) with a put option to provide a floor under the value.[4] Since a put option is essentially a levered short position, the future of these and similar investment vehicles would be in doubt if short sales were prohibited. The other major source of stock loans is the broking community, who would probably be forced to respond to a ban with higher charges, making it more costly to trade shares on the market. The net outcome would almost certainly be to reduce the attractiveness of saving in the form of equities.

Why do hedge funds sell short?

Many financial institutions are formally or informally barred from taking short positions. The hedge fund sector owes its existence in large part to the need for investment vehicles operating outside this constraint.

If a hedge fund manager views two firms trading on widely differing

---

3   New York's state pension fund said it would cease lending stocks in nineteen firms to short sellers on a temporary basis (BBC, 19 September 2008), but it remains to be seen whether other pension funds on either side of the Atlantic will want to follow this lead.

4   In this case, short positions and long positions can often complement each other so that their combined effect is simply a reduced long position. A ban on short sales would prevent a perfectly legitimate way of developing products for retail customers that provide equity exposure with some risk protection.

earnings multiples[5] as broadly comparable, he or she will conclude that the more expensive share is overpriced relative to the cheaper. If the fund manager has no particular reason to believe that one or the other is mispriced in absolute terms (i.e. relative to the market as a whole), the appropriate response is to buy the cheaper and sell short the dearer share. Notice that there are two reasons why simply buying the cheaper share is unsatisfactory. First, the proceeds of the short sale pay for the long position in the underpriced share, so that the net cost of the strategy is zero. Second, simply buying the supposedly under-priced share will leave the investor vulnerable to a fall in the market as a whole. This point is worth emphasising. If the fund manager can only take a long position, the trade could lose money even if his perception of mispricing turns out to be totally vindicated. For example, the 'under-priced' share may fall by 5 per cent while the 'overpriced' falls by 15 per cent, thereby vindicating the conjecture that the price of the dearer share was 10 per cent higher than it ought to have been relative to the cheaper. In these circumstances, the long position in the underpriced share *on its own* will have lost 5 per cent, whereas selling the overpriced share short and using the proceeds to buy the underpriced share will generate a 10 per cent profit.

The consequences of a short sales ban are therefore not as straight-forward as the overpricing of shares. In the example just quoted, if the fund manager is deterred from trading by the short sales prohibition and the additional risk it implies, the outcome is the persistence not of absolute overpricing, but of distortion to relative prices, which serves to keep some shares at too high and some at too low a price.

The net effect of deterring trades of this kind is first of all to block or slow down the process of price formation, distorting relative prices and the signals they send to savers and hence to the real economy. In addition, the lower volume of trade is likely to mean lower levels of liquidity, potentially making prices more, not less, volatile.

---

5   That is the ratios of their share prices to annual earnings – a commonly used measure of value.

A ban on short selling: who benefits?

If the opponents of short selling were restricted to the tabloid press, the furore might have been forgotten as quickly as the latest sensations in reality TV. In the event, however, the issue finds support from a more powerful, less fickle lobby. Not surprisingly, a ban on short sales is popular in the boardrooms of many UK quoted companies, where the idea of markets as elections in which short sellers are free to vote against the management is anathema – far better in their view to restrict the electorate to a Yes (purchase) or an abstention (no purchase). The fact that a ban may deter shareholders from buying in the first place, or indeed may convince savers they should avoid the stock market altogether, seems less important to them, since it represents no immediate threat to their positions.

The argument is totally self-serving, implying as it does that the loss of confidence in, for example, two of the UK's biggest banks during the autumn of 2008 was the result of a dastardly conspiracy by short-selling hedge funds, rather than of the market's realisation that gross mismanagement would make it impossible for them to survive without assistance on an enormous scale. Indeed, if short sellers are guilty of anything, it is that they failed to act sooner and in greater numbers. In the spring of 2007, when RBS and Barclays were locked in their battle for ownership of ABN Amro, a wave of short selling might have scuppered the disastrous takeover. As UK taxpayers, we may well ask the short sellers: where were you when we needed you most? In fact, reckless empire-building has been the bane of capitalism for some decades now (and has usually destroyed shareholder value, as academic economists have shown). It is paradoxical, however, that in the present climate there is so much opposition to mega-mergers, but so little support for the short selling that might help put an end to them.

In the end, there is only one answer to institutions that claim their share prices have been unduly driven down by short sellers: if you are so convinced they are underpriced, then for heaven's sake, fill your boots! That will solve the underpricing problem, make a substantial profit for yourself and/or your company, and at the same time impose crippling losses on the short sellers. Their failure to do so speaks volumes.

11 RATINGS AGENCIES, REGULATION AND FINANCIAL MARKET STABILITY

Alan D. Morrison

One of the most striking features of the current financial crisis has been the realisation that many structured financial products are far less safe than they appeared to be. Investors who relied upon creditworthiness assessments made by the major credit ratings agencies have seen their investments in complex structured financial products drop sharply in value. On 16 August 2008, Moody's downgraded 691 mortgage-backed bonds – that is, bonds that were collateralised by a claim on the cash flows generated by a portfolio of mortgage loans.[1] Over two thousand securities, mostly mortgage-backed, were downgraded in November 2007 alone; of these, 500 were downgraded more than ten notches on the standard ratings scale.[2] And the investors affected by the ratings agencies' downgrades were apparently sophisticated: for example, the *Financial Times* points to credit ratings cuts as one of the events that necessitated the US government's intervention in the insurance group AIG.[3]

Commentators and policymakers are eager to assign blame for the crisis, and the credit ratings agencies appear to be a convenient scapegoat. Henry Waxman, chair of the US House of Representatives' Oversight Committee, remarked recently that 'The credit rating agencies occupy a special place in our financial markets. The ratings agencies broke this bond of trust.'[4] How justified is this criticism? If the ratings

---

1   Sam Jones, 'How Moody's faltered', *Financial Times*, 17 October 2008.
2   Paul J, Davies, 'CDO downgrades break new records', *Financial Times*, 13 December 2007.
3   Aline van Duyn, 'Influence of ratings agencies questioned', *Financial Times*, 17 September 2008.
4   Alan Beattie, 'Credit agencies "broke bond of trust"', *Financial Times*, 22 October 2008.

agencies did fail to do their jobs properly, did they do so because of incompetence, did they respond to heightened competition by indulging in a race to the bottom, or were they just unlucky? And should we respond, as several members of the commentariat have suggested, by regulating their actions?

Credit ratings agencies sell opinions. So do newspapers. It would be illiberal and wrong headed to regulate newspapers; an argument for regulation of ratings agencies should be founded on a stronger argument than the observation that, post hoc, it appears that their opinions were incorrect. We need to understand how the agencies came to occupy a position of such prominence in the capital markets, and why their opinions are able to move markets so sharply. I will argue in this chapter that, in fact, the problem may be *too much* regulation of the agencies. It is certainly too soon to form a considered judgement on the failings, if any, of the market in securitised debt, and it would be a mistake to make substantial changes to the financial landscape based upon a shallow analysis of the problems that we currently face.

I begin my analysis by discussing the evidence that ratings were incorrectly assigned, and that the relationship between securitised bond prices and their ratings was confused.

The information content of bond ratings

Credit ratings are intended to give putative investors a simple indicator of the creditworthiness of the institutions and the bonds in which they invest. A credit rating is a letter-based code: the precise code employed depends upon the firm selling the code; the highest-rated bonds are usually assigned an Aaa or AAA code ('treble-A' rating), and the lowest-rated bonds a C code. Bonds rated at or above Baa or BBB are usually referred to as 'investment-grade'; weaker bonds are 'junk'. In theory, a ratings agency economises upon information production: it can generate information useful to many investors, so reducing duplication costs and hence the costs of capital market access.

There is a good deal of evidence that market prices move in response to credit ratings changes. For example, recent work by Norden and Weber (2004) and Hull et al. (2004) finds that the prices of credit default swaps move sharply in response to changes in the ratings of the obligor firms. Kilger and Sarig (2000) examine the 1982 refinement of Moody's bond rating system, which occurred without a prior market announcement and without any fundamental change in issuer risk, and find that, although the refinement did not change the total market value of borrowers, it *did* alter the split between debt and equity valuations.

Might the market sensitivity of market prices to market ratings reflect an excessive reliance upon ratings by market investors? This suggestion is of particular relevance in the market for the types of complex securities that have been associated with the current crisis. And there is plenty of evidence to support it that, if not conclusive, is at least highly suggestive. For example, we know from work by Matt Cuchra (2005) that about three-quarters of the yield variation on these complex securities reflects variation in their ratings. This suggests that investors are basing their investment decisions almost entirely upon rating data.

If investors base their investment decisions upon ratings, bond issuers will naturally attempt to game the system by structuring their bonds in order to obtain the highest possible rating. This type of structuring is easiest to accomplish when issuing securities such as the mortgage-backed bonds that have filled so many column inches of late: issuers can pick and choose their mortgages, and the structuring of the cash-flow streams that they generate, so as to generate the highest possible rating as cheaply as possible.

There is academic and anecdotal evidence to support this statement. For example, Benmelech and Dlugosz (2008) analyse a large universe of loan-backed bonds ('collateralised loan obligations', or 'CLOs'), and find a very high degree of uniformity in their design. This suggests strongly that bonds were constructed to fit a ratings agency template. Benmelech and Dlugosz discuss anecdotal evidence that the model used by Standard and Poor's (S&P), a major ratings agency, was widely known to bond issuers, who used S&P software to evaluate their issues before submitting them for rating.

Too much maths, not enough economics

Of course, it is not illegal to share one's opinions, and the way in which one arrives at them, with others. Indeed, current proposals for rating agency regulation stress the need for transparency in this area.[5] But information sharing in this context has a powerful effect: when everyone uses the same models, everyone makes the same mistakes. What were the effects of convergence upon a single, ratings-based approach to pricing?

Ratings are supposed to tell us the likelihood that a bond will make the repayments that it promised on time, and in full. The precise interpretation of this statement varies from one agency to another: Brennan et al. (2008) report that Standard and Poor's and Fitch base their ratings entirely upon default probabilities, while Moody's attempt to incorporate a measure of expected repayment levels in the wake of default.

Notwithstanding minor differences of definition, all of the ratings have one feature in common: they fail to distinguish between defaults that occur during economic booms, and those that occur during downturns. These default events are not the same thing: default hurts more when it comes in lean times than in times of plenty, and bonds that are relatively more likely to default in lean times should be worth more. But, when prices are based upon ratings that fail to distinguish between pro-cyclical and counter-cyclical default, they fail to reflect the difference between the two.

The effect outlined in the previous paragraph is the basis of a huge literature in the economics of asset pricing, and is one of the first things that an MBA student learns about finance and investments. It seems remarkable that a professional investor could be so foolish as to neglect

5   See Nikki Tait, 'Brussels set to clamp down on ratings agencies', *Financial Times*, 13 November 2008.

it. But evidence in recent papers by Coval et al. (2007, 2008) indicates that this is precisely what investors in structured finance have been doing. Investors have been buying mortgage-backed bonds and related securities at yields that are nowhere near enough to compensate them for the risks that they are taking. Brennan et al. (2008) provide evidence that issuers understand this, and that they structure their bonds accordingly.

Ratings agencies do not pretend to account for the cyclicality of default, so, arguably, investors are at fault when they fail adequately to account for it when selecting investments. But ratings agency methods have also been criticised of late. Benmelech and Dlugosz (2008) examine almost four thousand structured bonds that are backed by loan portfolios; the average rating of the loan collateral is B+, a 'junk' rating, while 70 per cent of the bonds are rated AAA, which is the highest possible investment grade. Issuers appear to be turning base metal into gold. Coval et al. (2008) show that, indeed, the ratings assigned require the ratings agencies to be 'extraordinarily confident' of their ability to estimate the default risk of the collateral loans, and the likelihood that these defaults would be correlated. They illustrate their argument by citing a 2007 conversation between Robert Rodriguez, the CEO of First Pacific Advisors, and Fitch, during which Fitch told Rodriguez that a 2 per cent fall in the US residential property market would be sufficient to causes losses to holders of the AAA tranches in mortgage-backed bonds.

The heroic assumptions upon which structured product ratings have relied were particularly apparent in the market for Constant Proportion Debt Obligations (CPDOs), a complex structure created in 2006 by the Dutch bank ABN Amro, and subsequently adopted by several other issuers.[6] These AAA-rated securities initially paid a return of 2 per cent over the standard interbank LIBOR rate, at a time when the corresponding spread for most AAA-rated corporate bonds was less than 0.2 per cent. Their launch was greeted with incredulity by several market

---

6   See Teklos et al. (2006) for a discussion of CPDO structures.

commentators: for example, Janet Tavakoli, an experienced securitisation consultant, is quoted in the *Financial Times* as saying that 'once again, the ratings agencies have proved that when it comes to some structured credit products, a rating is meaningless'.[7]

Notwithstanding comments like Tavakoli's, the market lapped up CPDOs. In fact, it transpired later that their ratings rested not only upon optimistic modelling assumptions, but also upon errors in computer code. Moody's reported early in 2009 that it was beginning disciplinary action against some of its staff after learning that a computer error had caused it to rate around $1 billion complex securities incorrectly.[8]

At first blush, it appears that market participants lost sight of the economics underlying the bond structures that they traded. The complex models that physicists and mathematicians build, for use in their own fields, are based upon parameters that we can measure: the strength of a gravitational field, the wavelength of infrared light, the speed at which sound travels, and so on. The models upon which securitisation ratings were based had a similar flavour: they used estimates of default rates, correlations of default, sectoral correlations and so on to generate statements about the properties of the cash flows generated by portfolios of mortgages and other loans. But, unlike the models of fluid mechanics from which credit analysis borrows much of its mathematics, the inputs for securitisation models reflect social decisions, which change when we measure them, and use them to guide our decision-making. It seems that many market participants emphasised the mathematics of their models at the expense of the economic phenomena that they were attempting to capture.

I do not believe that we can write this behaviour off as symptomatic of market irrationality, of excessive hubris or as the consequence of naturally short-termist thinking that should be checked by legislation.

7   Sam Jones, Gillian Tett and Paul J. Davies, 'CPDOs expose ratings flaw at Moody's', *Financial Times*, 20 May 2008.

8   Sam Jones and Gillian Tett, 'Moody's to investigate staff over rating bug', *Financial Times*, 1 July 2008.

Market players are seldom stupid; they respond rationally to the incentives that they face and, if we want to understand their behaviour, we need also to understand their incentives.

Credit ratings, regulation, and incentives

Prior to 1970, credit ratings were paid for by investors. Under this system, small investors could free-ride upon ratings paid for by larger investors, and, as a result, it was not economic to rate some issues. In the wake of the surprise 1970 Penn Central failure, investors started to demand ratings, and issuers started to pay for them.[9] This system is now the norm.

Payment by issuers for their own ratings generates an obvious conflict of interest. When a ratings agency relies for fees upon the firm whose creditworthiness it evaluates, one might expect it to lower its standards so as to increase the level of business it generates. The counter-argument rests upon reputational considerations. Agencies have nothing to sell if they lose their reputation for honesty in ratings and hence, goes the argument, they will resist the short-term incentive to race their competitors to the bottom in order to protect their long-run revenue stream.

Whether the short-run race-to-the-bottom effect or the long-run reputational effect dominates depends on the power of the short-term incentive to burn reputation. If the immediate profits from doing so are large enough, and the long-term profits to be obtained from maintaining a good reputation are sufficiently small, then it is rational to run down a reputation.[10] On the other hand, it would be surprising if rational investors did not anticipate the trade-off faced by the ratings agencies, and respond to a weakening of reputational incentives by reducing the credence they attached to credit ratings. If, as has been suggested, the conflict of interest faced by ratings agencies caused a diminution

---

9   See Cantor and Packer (1994).
10 See Morrison and Wilhelm (2007: chs 8 and 9) for a detailed analysis of this trade-off.

in standards in recent years, we have to ask ourselves why investors continued to take their ratings seriously.

One answer might be that opinions regarding creditworthiness ratings represent only a part of the services that ratings agencies provide to investors. This suggestion is not entirely new. The 1909 foundation of John Moody's railroad bond-rating business is usually regarded as marking the start of the credit ratings industry,[11] but Carruthers and Cohen (2006) study credit assessments made by antecedent businesses in the last two decades of the nineteenth century. They find little evidence that these assessments accurately predicted insolvency. They suggest a number of other explanations for the nineteenth-century use of credit ratings, including their use to provide scientific legitimacy for unscientific investment decisions.

Carruthers and Cohen's suggestion that ratings legitimise investment decisions has a clear parallel in today's financial markets. Cantor et al. (2007) report the results of a survey of 200 pension plan sponsors and investment managers in the USA and Europe, and find that 75 per cent face minimum rating requirements for their investments. In other words, if I create a security backed by a sub-investment-grade bond and a government security, I can sell it to the investment manager if the combination of these bonds has a BBB rating; he cannot avoid paying my fees by purchasing the two bonds for himself.

Ratings also play an increasingly important role in bank regulation. A 1936 announcement by the US Comptroller of the Currency referred banks to the ratings agencies to determine which bonds were speculative-grade and, hence, should not form a part of their portfolios (Portnoy, 1999). More recently, new bank capital regulations rely upon ratings.[12]

The adoption of ratings-based criteria in financial market regulation had a laudable goal: to make better use of market-generated data in

---

11 Sylla (2002) presents a clear history of credit ratings. The businesses studied by Carruthers and Cohen (2006) are characterised by Sylla as 'credit reporting agencies'.

12 See the Basel Committee on Banking Supervision (2006).

regulation. But it had an unintended consequence. When ratings were unregulated, all that the agencies had to sell was their opinion, and they therefore guarded their reputations jealously. The consequence was careful and conservative rating.

As Portnoy (1999, 2001) notes, when investment choices are restricted by ratings, agencies serve as gatekeepers. They sell admission to the regulated investment management and banking markets. In heavily regulated markets, this admission is worth more to issuers than the accuracy of ratings. In other words, introducing a regulator serves to *reduce* the value of the ratings agency's reputation; regulated agencies are more concerned with maintaining their licence to operate than their reputation for probity. Provided it does not endanger this licence, the rating agency's most rational action is to charge high fees to assist issuers in their search for strong ratings. I have already argued that this is precisely what the agencies did in the first seven years of this decade.

In short, when regulators use ratings to observe markets, they alter issuer and investor behaviour, and they alter the nature of the rating. Mathematical models based upon pre-regulation data cease to be accurate, because this data reflects a different playing field, not an eternal verity. But, in a regulated ratings market with restricted entry, I have argued that concern for accuracy is reduced. Using market data in regulation distorts the data.

Furthermore, regulatory reliance upon ratings has knock-on competitive effects. If regulators choose to rely upon credit ratings then, naturally, they will wish to screen the ratings agencies. In the USA, the approved regulators are the Nationally Recognised Statistical Rating Organisations (NRSROs); of the seven NRSROs, the largest three (S&P, Moody's, Fitch) account for over 90 per cent of the market. The Bank for International Settlements (Basel Committee on Banking Supervision, 2006) has published detailed criteria that national governments should use to screen putative new agencies.

Regulators use standard accepted rating methodologies to screen potential entrants into the ratings market. New ideas struggle to get a hearing in this type of market: fewer 'opinions' are expressed, and trust in the uniform, focal-point 'opinion' is greater. A regulatory barrier to entry prevents the type of methodological experimentation that might have prevented the problems I have already highlighted: the market's role as a discovery mechanism is undermined.

Conclusion

Ratings, particularly ratings for structured products, have been inaccurate. Regulations that rely upon credit ratings have therefore been ineffective, and have had the perverse effect of making ratings less reliable. A natural response by regulators and politicians is to increase the level of regulatory oversight on ratings agencies: this is precisely the strategy that Charlie McCreevy, the EU internal market commissioner, is advocating.[13] But I have argued that many of the recent problems in the market for credit ratings have arisen because of the ways in which ratings are currently used by regulators. His proposal would most likely reduce competition and the variety of opinions offered even further.

It is far from clear that we can resolve a problem of over-regulation by creating more regulations. A more appropriate response might be to reduce the regulatory role of the agencies, and to allow free entry into the ratings industry. Ratings agencies would again sell expertise, not regulatory certification, and a competitive wind might blow some creative destruction through the ratings industry.

References

Basel Committee on Banking Supervision (2006), *Basel II: International Convergence of Capital Measurement and Capital Standards: A Revised Framework – Comprehensive Version*, Basel: Bank for International Settlements.

13   See note 5, and also 'EU clamps down on credit rating agencies', *International Herald Tribune*, 12 November 2008.

Benmelech, E. and J. Dlugosz (2008), 'The alchemy of CDO credit ratings', Working Paper, Harvard Business School.

Brennan, M. J., J. Hein and S.-H. Poon (2008), 'Tranching and rating', Working Paper, University of Manchester.

Cantor, R. and F. Packer (1994), 'The credit rating industry', *Federal Reserve Bank of New York Quarterly Review*, Summer, pp. 1–26.

Cantor, R., W. P. Gwilym and S. Thomas (2007), 'The use of credit ratings in investment management in the US and Europe', *Journal of Fixed Income*, 17(2): 13–26.

Carruthers, B. G. and B. Cohen (2006), 'The mechanization of trust: credit rating in 19th century America', Working Paper, Department of Sociology, Northwestern University.

Coval, J. D., J. W. Jurek and E. Stafford (2007), 'Economic catastrophe bonds', *American Economic Review*.

Coval, J. D., J. W. Jurek and E. Stafford (2008), 'The economics of structured finance', Working Paper, Harvard Business School.

Cuchra, F.-M. (2005), 'Explaining launch spreads on structured bonds', Mimeo, Saïd Business School, University of Oxford.

Hull, J. C., M. Predescu and A. White (2004), 'The relationship between credit default swap spreads, bond yields, and credit rating announcements', *Journal of Banking and Finance*, 28(11): 2789–811.

Kilger, D. and O. H. Sarig (2000), 'The informational value of bond ratings', *Journal of Finance*, 55(6): 2879–902.

Morrison, A. D. and W. J. Wilhelm, Jr (2007), *Investment Banking: Institutions, Politics, and Law*, Oxford: Oxford University Press.

Norden, L. and M. Weber (2004), 'Informational efficiency of credit default swap and stock markets: the impact of credit rating announcements', *Journal of Banking and Finance*, 28(11): 2813–43.

Portnoy, F. (1999), 'The Siskel and Ebert of financial markets? Two thumbs down for the credit rating agencies', *Washington University Law Quarterly*, 77(3): 619–712.

Portnoy, F. (2001), 'The paradox of credit ratings', Law and Economics Research Paper no. 20, University of San Diego School of Law.

Sylla, R. (2002), 'A historical primer on the business of credit ratings', in R. M. Levich, G. Majnoni and C. Reinhart (eds), *Ratings, Ratings Agencies and the Global Financial System*, New York: Kluwer Academic Publishers.

Teklos, P., M. Sandigursky and M. King (2006), 'CDOs: the new best seller?', Citigroup European Quantitative Credit Strategy and Analysis Report.

12 THE GLOBAL FINANCIAL CRISIS: THE ROLE OF FINANCIAL INNOVATION
David T. Llewellyn

Introduction and key themes

The current crisis is different from its predecessors for several reasons. It is global in nature; it focused initially upon a comparatively new set of financial instruments (notably credit-risk-shifting instruments) that had become a new feature in the world of banking; a wide range of different markets and asset classes has been affected; it has caused major disruption to wholesale financial markets in general and interbank markets in particular; and it has already transformed the financial landscape (for example, the demise of the independent investment bank model that had become a defining feature of Wall Street). Although the crisis has not been confined to a particular type of institution, the centrepiece has been the position of banks. Above all, the crisis has become systemic in nature.

In this chapter, we consider the role of financial innovation in the financial crisis. Other aspects of the crisis are examined in my chapter in Part Two of this monograph.

To set the scene, six structural changes in the global financial system determine the background:

- a defining feature of recent financial history has been the sharp rise in the pace of financial innovation;
- an increasing 'financialisation' of economies (indicated by sharp growth in the volume of financial assets and liabilities and in financial intermediation relative to GDP);
- a more market-centric structure of financial systems (that is, a

rise in the role of financial markets relative to institutions in the financial intermediation process);
- a sharp rise in the use of derivatives markets;
- so-called (and largely unregulated) 'shadow banks' (such as hedge funds and Structured Investment Vehicles (SIVs)) have emerged as significant new players in the financial intermediation process (Tett, 2008); and
- an increased globalisation of finance and financial markets and systems.

For the purposes of this chapter, financial innovation refers to instruments and institutions that purported to shift credit risk away from the originators of loans. In the process, new business models of banks emerged (such as originate-and-distribute) which exposed banks to low-probability but high-impact risks, failures of corporate governance, and weakening lending standards. All this in turn induced an underestimation and underpricing of risk. Credit derivatives in particular enabled credit risk to be shifted, traded, insured and taken by institutions without the need for them to make loans directly to borrowers. This, in turn, changed in an important way the underlying economics and traditional model of banking.

Financial innovation and efficiency

While the central theme is that financial innovation had a decisive role in the financial crisis, a sense of proportion is needed, as this is not to argue that such innovations have no benefits. On the contrary, appropriately used, the new instruments have the potential to enhance the efficiency of the financial system in the performance of its core functions and, therefore, of the economy more generally (Llewellyn, 2009a).

Specifically, financial innovation has the potential to lower the costs of financial intermediation and offer wider access to credit. It allows financial institutions to better match their portfolio preferences and allocate funds to their most efficient use. Some instruments allow risks to be more accurately priced and hence enable the financial system to contribute to greater resource efficiency in an economy. New instruments also created facilities for risk transfer and management, increased the liquidity of credit risk, and allowed risks in financial instruments to be unbundled (see Llewellyn, 2009b). It is important, therefore, not to 'throw the baby out with the bathwater' or to inhibit innovation making important contributions to the efficiency of the financial system.

Financial innovation and stability

In fact, despite recent events, there are several potential routes through which financial innovation might enhance the stability characteristics of the financial system, and through which structured finance may make financial systems more resilient to shocks:

- To the extent that financial instruments spread risks more widely within the system (and to those who are more willing and able to absorb them), stability is likely to be enhanced.
- In many ways, such credit-risk-shifting instruments enable banks to respond more easily to certain types of shocks. Greenspan (2002) remarks that:

  [these episodes] suggest a marked increase over the two or three decades in the ability of modern economies to absorb unanticipated shocks ... this has doubtless been materially assisted by the recent financial innovations that have afforded lenders the opportunity to become considerably more diversified and borrowers to become far less dependent on specific institutions or markets for funds.

- A further perspective has been offered by the Bank for International Settlements (BIS): 'The ability to switch smoothly between balance sheet financing and market-based financing contributes to the robustness of a financial system and improves its ability to deal with strain' (Knight, 2004).

The overall assessment of the former chairman of the Federal Reserve was that 'these increasingly complex financial instruments have especially contributed to the development of a far more flexible, efficient, and resilient financial system than existed just a quarter-century ago' (Greenspan, 2002).

Against this, others argue that they have the potential to undermine financial stability, not least because they facilitate substantial leveraging of risk. There is a degree to which the instruments that enhance efficiency might under some circumstances threaten financial stability. Borio (2008) suggests that three particular characteristics of these instruments may have contributed to the financial turmoil that has characterised banking and financial markets since the summer of 2007. Their payoffs may be highly non-linear (Fender et al., 2008) in that they tend to produce a steady stream of returns in calm times, but in bad times can produce disproportionately heavy losses. Second, the risk profile of structured products can be very different from that of traditional bonds in that they can be subject to high 'tail risks' (i.e. higher probability of large losses). Also, as noted by Fender and Kiff (2004), modelling the future default and risk profile of some structured instruments is subject to considerable uncertainty, not least because of the limitations of current valuation models, which often underestimate the correlation of related risks.

The Financial Stability Forum report (BIS, 2005) identifies three further issues with respect to the stability characteristics of credit derivatives. The first is whether they create a clean and total risk transfer. Second, whether all participants understand the full nature of the risks involved in derivative transactions. Third, whether they produce a concentration of risks either inside or outside the banking system. A key dimension is the extent to which credit derivatives achieve a genuine transfer of credit risk.

A possible resolution of this apparent conflict focuses on the nature of shocks, in that the increased use of derivative instruments (notably with respect to credit risk) may enhance the stability characteristics of the financial system in the face of small and low-correlated risks, while they may make the system more vulnerable to large systemic shocks such as the drying-up of liquidity in international markets as in the summer of 2007 and also in 2008. Rajan offers the following perspective: 'Have these undoubted benefits [of financial innovation] come at a cost? Have we unwittingly accepted a Faustian bargain, trading greater welfare most of the time for a small probability of a catastrophic meltdown?' (Rajan, 2005).

What is new in financial innovation: credit risk shifting

The extensive use of instruments for the shifting of credit risk is a recent development and raises particular issues. There is a clear difference between a bank protecting against market-price risk and protecting again credit risk. In the former case the risk associated with a price movement is not influenced by the behaviour of the protection buyer: the probability is exogenous to the bank. Issues of asymmetric information, adverse selection and moral hazard, therefore, do not arise. The probability of a currency depreciation or a rise in interest rates is not in any way determined by the fact that a bank might protect itself against these risks by, for instance, conducting forward transactions or buying option contracts.

Instruments designed to shift credit risk, however, raise different issues. The relationship between a credit risk protection buyer and seller is fundamentally different from that between two counterparties in a swap or forward transaction. One of the features of credit risk is an asymmetric information dimension in that the lender has more information about the quality of loans than does a protection seller or a purchaser of a bank's asset-backed securities. The traditional theory of banking is that this asymmetric information (and the potential for adverse selection and moral hazard) acts as a bar to credit insurance or the shifting of credit risk. As with standard insurance theory, there might be a potential for banks to deliberately select high-risk loans to be insured (adverse selection) and to deliberately make high-risk loans or to fail to monitor borrowers (moral hazard) because the credit risk is passed to others.[1]

A further issue is the extent to which complex instruments are fully understood by the transactors. New complex products might have consequences that are not fully understood by the initiators, users or regulators (Masala, 2007). The full risk implications of some instruments are sometimes determined by the application of complex mathematical models, and these have to be appreciated as much by the users as by the institutions and regulators. The FSA has argued (FSA, 2002 and 2008) that complexity and the lack of transparency of many credit derivatives instruments (and notably CDOs) make it difficult for investors to determine precisely how exposed they are to particular risks. In particular, losses may be determined by the correlations of the risks within the portfolio, and these are in practice difficult to calibrate. Furthermore, banks have also become less transparent in that it is difficult to know to what extent credit risks have been shifted or acquired in the market through, for instance, credit default swaps.

The true extent to which risks are shifted through various instruments may also be brought into question, most especially at times of systemic crisis as in the second half of 2007. In practice what appears to be a risk-shifting instrument may have limitations. Thus, in the turbulence of 2007 and 2008, many banks found that, in practice, credit risks had not been shifted because, for instance, they had committed lines of credits to their Special Purpose Vehicles (SPVs) and conduits which, because of funding difficulties, were subsequently called upon. Furthermore, because of funding problems, several banks were induced either to take back securitised assets on to their balance sheet, or were unable to securitise loans they had made in anticipation of securitisation.

---

1   Though, interestingly, standard economic theory suggests that this should stop the market in these risk-shifting industries from developing.

Risks from credit instruments – a summary

There are several asymmetric information risks attached to the change in the banking model implied by credit risk-shifting instruments. The underlying basis is that the initial lender is likely to have more information about borrowers and a greater capacity to conduct post-loan monitoring. Several problems in particular may arise:

- The enhanced leverage potential of some credit derivatives may increase the vulnerability of the financial system to certain types of shock.
- Credit derivatives tend to be inherently pro-cyclical by accentuating credit growth in the upswing of an economic cycle but equally accentuating the opposite trend in the downswing.
- The initiating bank may have an incentive to shift the risk on its existing low-quality loans (De Marzo and Duffie, 1999; Pennacchi, 1988).
- A potential *moral hazard* arises to the extent that, as a bank is able to shift credit risk, it has less incentive to accurately assess risk. This problem surfaced in the US sub-prime mortgage market during 2007.
- There is less incentive to subsequently monitor the borrower (Gorton and Pennacchi, 1995; Morrison, 2005) and it is unlikely that sellers of credit risk protection (or buyers of CDOs) are able to monitor borrowers because they do not have the information or relationship advantages possessed by the initiating bank. This amounts to a new banking model which, to some extent, abrogates two of the fundamental roles of a bank: *ex ante* assessment of risk and *ex post* monitoring. For empirical evidence, see Mian and Sufi (2008) and Key et al. (2008)
- A lemons problem can emerge in some credit-risk transfer arrangements in that a lender buys protection on low-quality assets which may drive up the cost of protection on high-

quality assets (Duffie and Zhou, 2001). The standard lemons problem is that, in the presence of asymmetric information, a market may eventually break down as only low-quality assets are offered for protection (Akerlof, 1970).

- In some cases, either the borrower or the credit risk protection buyer may be able to influence the probability of a relevant 'credit event'.
- The risk shedder may retain a relationship with the borrower as an agent of the risk taker after the credit risk has been shifted. As noted in BIS (2003), this gives rise to a potential principal-agent problem. This leads to the question, in whose interest is the bank working?

Risk analysis: shifting versus changing

The financial crisis has revealed two major implications of credit-risk-shifting instruments. First, in many cases such risk was not in practice shifted to the extent that banks thought would be the case. Second, even when credit risk was shifted this was sometimes at the cost of increasing market, liquidity and ultimately funding risk. In effect, credit risk that is initially shifted may involuntarily come back on to the balance sheet of the originating bank. There are several possible reasons for this: a bank's SIV may be unable to continue issuing asset-backed commercial paper; loans that were planned to be securitised may prove to be 'non-securitisable' because of funding constraints; the originating bank may be called upon to honour agreed lines of credit to SIVs, and a bank may be induced to take back on to its balance sheets securitised assets in order to prevent a potential reputation risk.

In the case of Northern Rock (but also several other banks) the use of credit-risk-shifting instruments exposed the bank to a low-probability but high-impact risk in that the reliance on short-term wholesale market funding to finance long-term mortgages meant that the bank became structurally dependent on a limited number of markets for its funding (Llewellyn, 2007). It was always judged that the drying up of all these markets at the same time would be extremely unlikely in that it had seldom, if ever, happened before. Equally, however, it would be very serious if this were to occur. In the event, this is precisely what did happen. Such risks equally applied to institutions and investors who would issue short-term commercial paper in order to acquire asset-backed securities of various kinds.

Problems are compounded in the case of many derivative instruments by the fact that they can become difficult to price, not least because the risk characteristics are opaque and complex. When secondary markets dried up in these instruments after the summer of 2007, prices became unavailable. This forced holders (banks) to attempt to value their holdings of derivative instruments on the basis of models that were found to be fundamentally flawed in two respects: they were based on an insufficiently long observation period from which to calculate probabilities, and they did not take sufficient account of the tail-risk that the risks attached to the assets within CDOs might themselves be highly correlated. Thus what were thought to be diversified instruments turned out to be highly concentrated.

Financial innovation and a new economics of banking: the ultimate cause of the crisis

Our central theme has been that the emergence of new banking models proved to be a major factor in the emergence of the current crisis. Five particular trends are identified:

- The growth in bank assets has been substantially in excess of the rise in bank deposits.
- The rise in bank loans has substantially exceeded the rise in banks' risk-weighted assets.
- There has been a sharp rise in the proportion of investment and trading activity in banks' balance sheets relative to loans.

- There has been an increased dependency on money market funding and funding through securitisation models.
- There has been a powerful trend towards using credit derivatives as a means of supposedly shifting credit risk.

With respect to the last-mentioned, the key issue is that securitisation and the use of credit-risk-shifting instruments came to be strategic within banks rather than marginal: their use became excessive and an integral part of banks' business models.

In some important respects, financial innovation (and most especially the emergence of credit derivatives) has changed the underlying economics of banking. Banks traditionally have information, risk analysis and monitoring advantages which enable them to solve asymmetric information problems and hence mitigate adverse selection and moral hazard (Llewellyn, 2009b). In this standard model, banks accept deposits and use their comparative advantages to transform deposits into loans. The bank accepts the credit (default) risk, holds the asset on its own balance sheet, monitors its borrowing customers, and holds appropriate levels of capital to cover unexpected risk. It also internally insures its loans through the risk premia incorporated into the rate of interest on loans. In this process, the bank offers an integrated service in that it performs all the core functions in the financial intermediation process.

Furthermore, in this traditional model the bank is not able to shift credit risk to other agents because of its asymmetric information advantages: a potential buyer or insurer of a loan from a bank might judge that, because of the bank's information advantage, there is an adverse selection and moral hazard potential in that the bank might select low-quality loans to pass on and, if it knew that it could pass on risk, it might be less careful in assessing the risk of new loans and would conduct less intensive monitoring of borrowers after loans have been made. For the same reason, the traditional view of the bank is that it is unable to externally insure its credit risks and instead applies a risk (insurance) premium on loans to cover expected risks and holds capital as an internal insurance fund to cover unexpected risks. In this traditional view of the bank, therefore, credit risk cannot be shifted or insured, there is no liquidity to bank loans, and banks are locked into their loan portfolios. Banks therefore have the incentive both to be careful in the loans they make and to monitor borrowers after loans have been made.

Many aspects of this traditional model, however, came to be questioned. In the securitisation model the process of securitisation (including via CDOs) means that the bank is able to sell loans and hence the bank does not hold the loan on its own balance sheet, does not absorb the credit risk, and hence does not need to hold capital against the credit risk. This depends, however, upon precisely how the securitisation is conducted and most especially whether the SPV is truly bankruptcy-remote from the bank and vice versa.

The credit default swap model is similar to the securitisation model except that, while the credit risk is passed to the protection seller, the asset remains on the balance sheet of the originating bank. Furthermore, in this model there is explicit external insurance of bank loans.

Under the new model, the bank is no longer required to perform all the functions in the bank intermediation business. Credit risk transfer facilities and instruments change the relationship between borrowers and lenders and create different incentive structures to those contained in the traditional model of the banking firm.

Credit-risk-shifting derivatives contributed to the sharp growth of credit by many banks. In addition, however, banks stopped behaving as banks in the traditional way and, in effect, came to act as brokers between ultimate borrowers and those who either purchased asset-backed securities or who offered CDS insurance.

Conclusion

Financial innovation has become a defining characteristic of financial systems over recent years. In the process it has contributed, in some countries more than others, to major structural change to bank models, the structure of financial systems and to more integration between systems. Knight (2004) has argued that the transformation of the financial landscape has altered the nature of risk. The reverse causation can also be argued: that new instruments have themselves been a force in the transformation of the financial landscape.

Over the past decade, banks have considerably enhanced their risk analysis and management systems, and financial innovation has contributed to this in a significant way. For a decade or more, such innovation developed in a scenario of strong growth in the world economy, a fairly stable economic and monetary environment, low credit risks, and stable and low interest rates. The experience of the current financial crisis indicates, however, that techniques and instruments that purport to shift credit risk in a stable environment may become problematic when the market environment becomes more volatile and uncertain, and when there are systemic shocks, most especially when they involve low-probability but high-impact risks. In this sense, some risk-shifting innovations are 'fair weather' friends.

The financial crisis followed a period of several years during which banks had experienced exceptionally benign market conditions, which had the effect of generating rapid and substantial growth of business, enabling banks to diversify their business structures, generating new business models, and ushering a period of exceptionally high profitability. The period 2000 to 2007 was, in many countries, the most profitable period for banks in particular and the financial sector in general. The fallout from the most serious financial crisis since the Great Depression is, however, likely to reverse many of these trends and force a rethink of business models. The traditional textbook model of a bank, whereby it makes loans, keeps the asset on the balance sheet, holds capital against the risk, and is unable to externally insure its credit risk, seemed to have evaporated with the experience of the early years of this century. Banks managed to do what the traditional textbook model said was not possible – though these new models were untested in difficult economic conditions, until recently.

As, to some extent, the crisis is a product of banks not behaving like banks, perhaps the traditional textbook model was right after all. It is notable that opinions on the risks of new models of banking were divided and that many, including in central banks and regulators, believed that banking risks would be more widely dispersed and less systemic. Regulators were not ahead of the curve. The new model of banking appears to have been very costly. Shareholders of some banks have lost more or less all of their capital. There is little reason to suppose that, as with all market innovations, the market will not resolve the problem, either by adjusting the new model or by returning to more traditional models of banking.

References

Akerlof, G. (1970), 'The market for lemons: quality uncertainty and the market mechanism', *Quarterly Journal of Economics*, 84(3): 488–500.

BIS (2003), *Credit Risk Transfer*, Basel: Committee on the Global Financial System, Basel, January.

BIS (2005), *Credit Risk Transfer*, Basel: Committee on the Global Financial System, Basel, March.

Borio, C. (2008), 'The financial turmoil of 2008–?: a preliminary assessment and some policy considerations', BIS Working Paper no. 251, Basel: BIS, March.

De Marzo, P. and D. Duffie (1999), 'A liquidity-based model of security design', *Econometrica*, January, pp. 65–99.

Duffie, G. R. and C. Zhou (2001), 'Credit derivatives in banking: useful tools for managing risk', *Journal of Monetary Economics*, 48: 25–54.

Fender, I. and J. Kiff (2004), 'CDO rating methodology: some thoughts on model risk and its implications', BIS Working Paper no. 163, November.

Fender, I., N. Tarashev and H. Zhu (2008), 'Credit fundamentals, ratings and value-at-risk CDOs versus corporate exposures', *BIS Quarterly Review*, March.

FSA (Financial Services Authority) (2002), *Cross-Sector Risk Transfer*, London: FSA, May.

FSA (2008), *Financial Risk Outlook*, London: FSA.

Gorton, G. and G. Pennacchi (1995), 'Banks and loan sales: marketing non-marketable assets', *Journal of Monetary Economics*, 35: 389–411.

Greenspan, A. (2002), 'International financial risk management', Remarks to the Council on Foreign Relations, Washington, DC, November.

Key, B., T. Mukherjee, A. Seru and V. Vig (2008), 'Did securitisation lead to lax screening?: evidence from the sub-prime loans 2001–6', http//ssrn.com/abstract=1093137, January.

Knight, M. (2004), 'Markets and institutions: managing the evolving financial risk', 25th SUERF Colloquium, Bank for International Settlements, Basel, October.

Llewellyn, D. T. (1999), *The New Economics of Banking*, SUERF Study no. 5, Vienna: SUERF.

Llewellyn, D. T. (2007), 'The Northern Rock failure: a crisis waiting to happen', *Journal of Financial Regulation and Compliance*, December.

Llewellyn, D. T. (2009a), 'Financial innovation and the global financial crisis', in S. Mollentze (ed.), *Monetary Policy in South Africa*, Proceedings of the 2008 South African Reserve Bank Conference, South African Reserve Bank, Pretoria.

Llewellyn, D. T. (2009b), 'The new banking and financial system', in D. Mayes, R. Pringle and M. Taylor (eds), *New Frontiers in Regulation and Oversight of the Financial System*, London: Central Banking Publications.

Masala, F. (2007), 'Recent financial innovations and their implications for risk management', Report for the 2007 Advisory Board meeting of the European Banking Report Observatory, Italian Bankers Association, Rome, November.

Mian, A. and A. Sufi (2008), 'The consequences of mortgage credit expansion: evidence from the 2007 mortgage default crisis', http//ssm.com/abstract=1072304, January.

Morrison, A. D. (2005), 'Credit derivatives, disintermediation and investment decisions', *Journal of Business*, 78: 621–48.

Pennacchi, G. G. (1988), 'Loan sales and the cost of bank capital', *Journal of Finance*, 43: 375–96.

Rajan, R. G. (2005), 'Has financial development made the world riskier', Washington, DC: International Monetary Fund, August.

Tett, G. (2008), 'Leaders at wits' end as markets throw one tantrum after another', *Financial Times*, 11 October.

13 MORAL FAILURE: BORROWING, LENDING AND THE FINANCIAL CRISIS
Samuel Gregg

Introduction

A predictable by-product of the 2008 financial crisis was a renewed wave of moral condemnation of market capitalism, invariably from those who might be called 'the usual suspects'. Germany's finance minister at the time, for example, proclaimed that 'Anglo-Saxon' capitalism was finished. Not to be outdone, the Anglican Archbishop of York infamously likened the practice of short selling to the behaviour of 'bank-robbers'. Equally unsurprising was the near-universal insistence of leaders of governments and international organisations around the world that the key to resolving the financial crisis and preventing similar occurrences in the future was to increase the regulation of banks and the financial industry.

Other commentators have highlighted the extent to which government regulation as well as political manipulation of the US sub-prime mortgage market actually played a major role in facilitating the financial meltdown (see the chapter by Butler). Much ink has been spilt detailing the role played by loose and poorly targeted monetary policy – especially by the Greenspan Federal Reserve – in allowing excessive amounts of cheap money to flow into and circulate through the US and therefore the global economy. Economists of the various neoclassical schools have focused heavily upon the macro-dimensions of the crisis.

If, however, we accept that the essence of economic activity consists of individuals and institutions making choices of a creative and reactive nature, then attention should also be directed to the manner in which credit has been requested and extended by borrowers and lenders throughout the world. In this regard, questions have been asked about the leverage ratios maintained by major financial houses and investment banks in the months preceding the crisis. There has, however, been rather more reluctance to analyse and critique the choices made by individual borrowers. This may have something to do with the general climate of moral relativism that discourages people from critiquing the choices of others in anything other than terms that conform to whatever happens to be politically correct or fits the *zeitgeist* of the moment. Thus, while various choices made by particular investment banks have been heavily – and, in many instances, rightly – criticised on moral and economic grounds, rather fewer moral critiques have been made of the behaviour of individuals who, for example, misrepresented – i.e. lied – about their assets, income and liabilities in order to obtain loans and mortgages. Base Point Analytics (2007; cf. Mayer et al., 2008), for example, found some degree of borrower misrepresentation in as many as 70 per cent of American early-payment defaults in a study of 3 million loans originated between 1997 and 2006. In other words, a good number of mortgage arrangements – many of which were used as the foundation for an increasing number of securities and equities – were based on untruths about assets and untruths about persons. Such actions are already illegal, so extra regulation is unlikely to deter future misrepresentation. Indeed, the only sure way to address this situation is for people to stop lying. Knowing and choosing the truth, it seems, is not as dispensable for harmonious human existence and economic relations as some imagine.

Not a new issue

A revealing feature of the analyses of the borrowing and lending habits contributing to aspects of the 2008 financial crisis is that they indirectly underline the extent to which many moral philosophers and economists have forgotten that the extension and seeking of credit were subjects of considerable and often heated discussion for centuries. The very morality of charging interest on loans has been intensely debated by religious and secular thinkers for over two thousand years. Indeed, Adam Smith actually favoured usury laws (Smith, 1984 [1776]: II.iv.14; cf. Paganelli, 2008). As John T. Noonan illustrates in his classic study of the Catholic Church's teaching on usury, Christianity's internal debate about this subject led to major clarifications of the nature of money, the development of the first 'embryonic theory of economics', and 'the first attempt at a science of economics known to the West' (Noonan, 1957: 2).[1]

In more recent years, political economists and historians of economic thought have illustrated that the entire practice of fractional reserve banking was condemned as immoral and profoundly disruptive of the social, legal and economic order from Roman times until approximately the seventeenth century. The moral error was considered to lie in 'the self-interested use, via the granting of loans to third parties, of money placed by bankers in demand deposits' (Huerta de Soto, 2008: 32). Jesús Huerta de Soto is one of a number of contemporary Austrian school economists who have illustrated how attention to the failure of banks to adhere to a 100 per cent reserve requirement plays a major role in the Austrian school's theory of credit and the business cycle.

Indispensable basic virtues

It may be the case that the relevance of this history for understanding aspects of the 2008 financial crisis and our ability to avoid similar difficulties in the future will become better understood with the passage of time. Of more immediate importance, however, may be a growing

---

1   Perhaps the twentieth century's foremost modern expert on the subject, Noonan famously concluded – *contra* the Archbishop of Canterbury's 2008 assertion that Christianity simply changed its position on moneylending in the sixteenth century – that the Catholic teaching on usury 'remains unchanged' (Noonan, 1957: 399). The sin of usury, Noonan states, was always and remains understood as 'the act of taking profit on a loan without just title' (ibid.: 399). Noonan then adds: 'What is just title, what is technically to be treated as a loan, are matter of debate, positive law, and changing evaluation. The development on these points is great. But the pure and narrow dogma is the same today as in 1200' (ibid.: 400).

realisation that if the benefits of borrowing and lending for individuals, institutions and society are to be best realised and extensive regulation avoided, then we may need to consider the economic significance – even indispensability – of particular moral habits, or what philosophers ranging from Aristotle to Smith called the virtues.[2]

Perhaps the most necessary such habit is the virtue of prudence.[3] The ancient Greeks, as well as medieval philosophers, viewed prudence as the cause and measure of all the non-theological virtues. It expresses the 'perfected ability' of individuals as creatures possessing right reason and free will to make morally correct practical decisions. An employee of a mortgage lender, for example, draws upon his experience and all the data available to him at a given moment and decides that it is beneficial to extend one person a mortgage while also deciding to deny another person's request for an extension of an existing loan. The employee's decisions are the product of an act of prudence (or imprudence), and may involve other virtues such as that of courage (taking a prudential risk on the successful borrower or turning down business that might increase the employee's sales figures on which his salary may be judged) and justice (reflecting carefully upon his decisions because it is what the employee owes in justice to his employer).

Similarly the borrower should act with prudence, making decisions based upon experience that do not lead to him being overstretched. It is often thought that many borrowers are too unsophisticated to act with prudence and that they need to be protected by regulation. Though prudence requires people to become informed, this need not involve becoming immersed in complex technical information. Tradition, rules of thumb and the observation of the behaviour of other sensible people have worked for many generations as a more than adequate control mechanism for keeping personal borrowing under control.

---

2   Archbishop Vincent Nichols, the Roman Catholic Archbishop of Westminster, is one of the few religious leaders who have underlined this point instead of arguing for more extensive regulation of the financial industry. See Nichols (2008).

3   This section of the chapter draws upon Gregg (2008).

Prudence has its own integral parts. Among other features, it includes an understanding of first principles (for example, 'don't steal'), open-mindedness, humility, caution, the willingness to research alternative possibilities, foresight, shrewdness, and the capacity to form an accurate sense of the reality of situations. Without gradually acquiring most or all of these qualities, it is arguable that someone working in the world of finance will either not last very long or will continue to make some very bad decisions. Prudence allows the practice and institutions of credit to play their indispensable role in the modern market economy. Similarly it is also clear that, without these qualities, householders who borrow will also make bad decisions which could have serious consequences, as well as become inclined to misrepresent their position to lenders.

Can we replace prudence with regulation?

Throughout the financial crisis, considerable anger has been directed against those who specialise in the credit business, especially sub-prime lending, be it of mortgages or credit cards. No doubt, some predatory lending has occurred. But why, some argue, should sub-prime-lending businesses exist in the first place? Are they not financial traps for the poor and vulnerable? Do they not discourage prudent saving? There have even been calls for official caps on interest rates offered by private lenders.

The difficulty with some such critiques is that they often reflect fundamental misunderstandings of the nature of credit and its underlying moral apparatus. Credit is about lending others financial means – the capital that most of us need at some point of our lives. Whether it is starting a business or buying a house, most people need capital. This means someone else such as a bank or a private lender has to be willing to take a risk. They do stand to profit if the mortgage is paid off or the business succeeds. But they also may lose if a house is foreclosed or a business goes bankrupt. Charging interest is how lenders maintain the value of their loans and make a profit (the margins of which are much narrower than most people realise), thereby increasing the sum total of capital available in a society. Interest is also a lender's way of calibrating risk: the higher the risk, the higher the interest rate necessary to compensate for the greater possibility of loss. It follows that if interest-rate ceilings were imposed by government fiat, lenders would effectively be prohibited from charging interest rates commensurate to the risks involved. Hence, they would be unlikely to lend capital to entrepreneurs and businesses pursuing high-risk endeavours. Many risky but wealth-creating and employment-generating activities would thus simply never occur. Legislated interest-rate ceilings would also mean that many people of lesser means would never have the chance to acquire the capital they may need, for example, to go to university or start a small business, let alone begin developing a credit record. Entire categories of people – recent immigrants, the urban poor – could be condemned to life on the margins.

But at a deeper level, we also forget that while credit is about capital, it is ultimately about something more intangible but nonetheless real. The word 'credit' is derived from *credere* – the Latin verb for 'to believe' but also 'to trust'. Thus, whether it is a matter of giving someone a credit card for the first time, or extending to a business the capital that it needs to grow into a great enterprise, providing people with credit means that you trust and believe in them enough to take a risk on their insight, reliability, honesty, prudence, thrift, courage, enterprise and, above all, their prudence: in short, the moral habits without which wealth creation cannot occur in the first place, let alone be sustained. A moment's thought about credit should therefore remind us how much market capitalism, so often derided as materialistic, relies deeply upon a web of moral qualities for its efficacy and sustainability. As the credit crunch has taught us, once these are corrupted – whether by basic dishonesty, excessive regulation or political manipulation of Fannie Mae and Freddie Mac proportions – the wheels of wealth creation shudder and eventually grind to a halt. Businesses die. People lose their jobs. Families suffer. It is simply the case that regulation and moral virtues have different functions. One cannot replace the other.

Conclusion

No one should doubt that the modern case for the free market economy, so painstakingly developed against interventionists of all stripes since Smith's time, has been set back years by the disarray in financial markets. The very same calamity, however, should remind everyone that loosening the political bonds imposed on economic liberty requires society's moral bonds to be constantly renewed and strengthened. In short, we are learning the hard way that virtues like prudence, temperance, thrift, promise-keeping and honesty (not to mention a willingness not to do to others what we would not want them to do to us) cannot be optional extras in communities that value economic freedom. If markets are going to work and appropriate limits on government power are to be maintained,[4] then societies require substantial reserves of moral capital. With so many people's economic wellbeing now partly determined by the decisions of those working in financial industries, the virtues (especially that of prudence) should be premium assets sought by banks and financial houses in their employees and directors. Classically understood, virtue ought to be pursued for the sake of human moral flourishing in itself. But this does not mean that we should close our eyes to the very real economic benefits and stability that may flow from larger numbers of people embracing the virtues. The same virtues are also required among consumers of financial products.

In the end, no amount of regulation – heavy or light – can substitute for the type of character formation that is supposed to occur in families, schools, churches and synagogues. These are the institutions (rather

---

4   This not to suggest that, in the absence of moral virtues in markets, a centrally planned economy will be better than a market system. It is just that the clamour for government intervention is that much greater and that much more difficult to resist in practice when markets are not grounded in virtue.

than ethics auditors and business ethics courses) which Adam Smith identified as primarily responsible for helping people develop what he called the 'moral sense' that causes us to know instinctively when particular courses of action are imprudent or simply wrong. At the end of his life, Adam Smith added an entirely new section entitled 'Of the character of virtue' to the sixth and final edition of his *Theory of Moral Sentiments*. His reasons for doing so are much debated. But perhaps Smith decided that as he glimpsed a world in which the spread of free markets was already beginning to diminish poverty, he needed to re-emphasise the importance of sound moral habits for societies that aspired to be both commercial and civilised. This surely is advice worth heeding today.

References

Base Point Analytics (2007), 'Early payment default – links to fraud and impact on mortgage lenders and investment banks', www.basepointanalytics.com/mortgagewhitepapers.shtml.

Gregg, S. (2008), 'Credit crunch, character crisis', Speech delivered to the Thomas More Institute and the ESCP-EAP European School of Management, 22 October.

Huerta de Soto, J. (2008), *The Austrian School: Market Order and Entrepreneurial Creativity*, Cheltenham: Edward Elgar.

Mayer, C. J., K. M. Pence and S. M. Sherlund (2008), *The Rise in Mortgage Defaults*, Washington, DC: Finance and Economics Discussion Series, Divisions of Research & Statistics and Monetary Affairs, www.federalreserve.gov/Pubs/feds/2008/200859/200859pap.pdf.

Nichols, V. (2008), 'Homily at civic mass, Sunday, 23 November 2008', www.birminghamdiocese.org.uk/assets/pdf/CIVIC per cent20MASS per cent202008.pdf.

Noonan, J. T. (1957), *The Scholastic Analysis of Usury*, Harvard, MA: Harvard University Press.

Paganelli, M. P. (2008), '*In Medio Stat Virtus*: an alternative view of usury in Adam Smith's thinking', in S. J. Peart and D. M. Levy (eds), *The Street Porter and the Philosopher*, Ann Arbor, MI: University of Michigan Press, pp. 202–27.

Smith, A. (1984) [1776], *An Inquiry into the Nature and Causes of the Wealth of Nations*, ed. R. H. Campbell, A. S. Skinner and W. B. Todd, Indianapolis: Liberty Classics.

PART TWO
THE REGULATORY RESPONSE

14 MORE REGULATION, LESS REGULATION OR BETTER REGULATION?

Philip Booth

Introduction

The crash has led to much comment on the need for changes in the way we regulate financial institutions. Unsurprisingly, economists such as Joseph Stiglitz have called for greater regulation of both financial products and financial market participants.[1] Will Hutton, in an open letter to David Cameron, apparently oblivious to the generally accepted economic history of the Great Depression, commented: 'I fear that, like Tony Blair, you shrink from the truth of the matter; that free and lightly regulated financial markets, upon which so much of our business elite's prosperity is dependent, have delinquent propensities for speculation and short-termism that profoundly damage the real economy. The crash of 2008–09, like 1929, is because once again we did not keep finance on a tight rein.'[2]

The EU, at its summit meeting on 22 February 2009, agreed to bring in a new charter to increase EU-wide regulation across all financial markets: including those hitherto largely unaffected by state regulation. This charter, if implemented, would lead to the regulation of all financial activities around the world, including those of credit-rating agencies. There was no questioning of whether increased regulation was the appropriate instrument to achieve the desired goals or of whether regulation could lead to the sort of unforeseen consequences discussed, for example, by Copeland and Morrison in Part One of this monograph.

---

1   See, for example, www.guardian.co.uk/commentisfree/cifamerica/2008/oct/22/economy-financial-crisis-regulation (accessed 19 February 2009).
2   See: www.guardian.co.uk/politics/2009/feb/01/will-hutton-david-cameron-debate (accessed 19 February 2009).

Indeed, it is difficult to see what problem EU leaders are trying to fix given that, as Beenstock pointed out in Part One, the regulated parts of financial markets have led to more systemic problems than more lightly regulated parts such as hedge funds.

UK opinion is not necessarily representative of the EU establishment. Some discussion has been quite reasoned. Even the Financial Services Authority's (FSA) own review of the Northern Rock crisis recommended only a strengthening of processes rather than a wholesale new approach to regulation (see Financial Services Authority, 2008), though it has recently described its former regulatory approach as 'light touch' and has promised to make participants in financial markets fear it from now on. There has been interesting and mature comment from some senior clergy. Archbishop Vincent Nichols of Birmingham, for example, commented: 'We have neglected the development of shared ethical values and principles to guide and shape our behaviour, believing that to be an unattainable goal, and we have substituted raft after raft of regulation.'[3] Perhaps wisely, Archbishop Nichols did not make his views on the future of financial regulation clear, but he obviously does not believe that regulation can perfect financial markets.

Participants in financial markets, regulators and politicians often focus on the need for 'better regulation'. This is a somewhat glib phrase that is convenient for politicians in that it does not create enemies. There are enemies of 'more regulation', there are enemies of 'less regulation', but who could oppose 'better regulation'? But perhaps better regulation is possible in the context of less regulation. What is really needed is an understanding of the economic events that led to the crash, and of the management of the crash itself by central bankers, governments, market participants and regulators, to develop some principles for the future of regulation. If we seek such an understanding, it becomes clear that the appropriate regulatory interventions could be very specific and much less intrusive than the current regulatory structure.

---

3   www.birminghamdiocese.org.uk/assets/pdf/CIVIC per cent20MASS per cent202008.
     pdf (accessed 24 February 2009).

Two things are clear from Part One. The extensive system of banking regulation coming from domestic, EU and international sources did not stop the crash of 2008 from happening. Second, even if regulators had had greater powers, they probably would not have used them to take actions to stop banks building up risky positions in securitised instruments and credit derivatives. Central bankers and regulators, as well as organisations such as the International Monetary Fund, were sanguine about the growth in complex financial products that occurred in the early part of the 21st century. Some of the chapters in Part One suggest that the regulators had, in fact, been captured by the industry.

Public choice economics

We should begin by examining some aspects of economic theory. Without reference to theory, supported by empirical observation, ideas about the future of regulation will simply be ad hoc and are likely to be dictated by preconceived ideas about the ability, or otherwise, of markets to regulate themselves.

It seems that many of the facts relating to the crash fit into the way of thinking of the public choice school of economics (see, for example, Tullock, 2006). It may be difficult for the casual observer to understand how regulators could simultaneously bind the financial sector up in detailed regulation – a feature of financial regulation in both the UK and the USA – and yet, when it comes to action to deal with an institution that is building up risks, be so lethargic. Public choice theory predicts that this is a likely outcome of giving regulators wide powers that are not well defined. Regulators will wish to build the size and power of their bureaus, which they can do by drafting handbooks of detailed regulation.[4] Regulators will also be risk averse and not wish to see a failure

---

4   It is not easy to navigate the FSA's handbooks. The main handbook for banks contains ten sections, however. We can drill down to get relevant information as in the following example. The section entitled 'Prudential standards' is divided into eleven subsections. The subsection 'Prudential sourcebook for banks, building societies and investment

on their 'watch'. This may well lead to them regulating firms to avoid risks building up (something that clearly did not happen in wholesale banking, though it happens on a grand scale in consumer finance), but, crucially and perhaps paradoxically, not intervening when risks materialise. The regulator faces incentives not to intervene when a financial company is facing trouble as the regulator may hope that the firm can trade its way back to solvency if investment markets move in its favour. If the firm does so successfully, those to whom regulators are accountable will be unaware that they have allowed a failure to happen. This means that when there are problems, and they fail to go away, they are likely to build up and possibly pose systemic risks.

The use of detailed but misdirected regulation is predicted by another aspect of public choice theory. This suggests that regulators can become captured by the regulated industry – this is particularly true if there is a substantial amount of employment traffic between the industry and the regulator. Detailed regulation suits the industry because it raises costs to potential rivals and competitor small firms. The lack of prompt action also suits the industry. As noted, delaying intervention allows a company to try to trade out of its difficulties, to the obvious advantage of shareholders (who have limited liability) and management (who may retain their jobs) but at a cost to the other creditors of the business, including depositors.

One might ask: why do the monitors of regulators not address these problems? Unfortunately, the monitors of regulators have no incentive to be well informed. Electors vote on a range of issues and have an infinitesimal chance of influencing an election. Politicians, in turn, respond

firms' is made up of fourteen sub-subsections. The sub-subsection 'Market risk' is divided into eleven sub-sub-subsections. The sub-sub-subsection on 'Interest rate PRR' has 66 paragraphs. This is known as 'principles-based regulation' by the FSA. As far as I could see, based on this example, there could be over 1,100,000 paragraphs: it is not feasible to count all the paragraphs and nor is it possible to download the whole book. Remarkably, I could find nothing on liquidity risk, the main failing of Northern Rock, though I am sure it must be addressed somewhere. See http://fsahandbook.info/FSA/html/handbook/BIPRU/7/2 (downloaded 19 February 2009).

to the incentives facing electors and also have little incentive to become well informed. It is ironic that regulators often talk about the need for regulation to overcome information asymmetries that exist within the financial system when there are such chronic incentives for such information asymmetries to exist within the regulatory system.

Finally, public choice economics, together with Austrian economics, points out that regulators cannot systematically correct market failures, even if there are times when regulation can theoretically improve on market outcomes. Regulators do not have the knowledge to create the conditions of a perfect market where those conditions do not exist in practice.

Public choice economics should, in the first place, lead us to have some humilty about what regulation can achieve. Second, it suggests that a narrow and specific regulatory remit will be more effective than a general remit to achieve widely defined objectives. This will be important for our discussion below.

Insights from Austrian economics

Austrian economics discusses how the continual process of competition leads to welfare enhancement through the discovery of new entrepreneurial opportunities (see, for example, de Soto, 2008). These entrepreneurial discoveries do not simply involve the development of new products or more efficient ways of producing products but also the development of new institutional approaches to overcome the obstacles to efficiency that neoclassical economists often suggest are permanent features of financial markets. Thus stock exchanges, professional standards, industry codes of conduct and rating agencies all exist to help, in their different ways, overcome problems caused by information asymmetries and the incentives to reckless behaviour that limited liability can provide. Furthermore, in a competitive market, financial services companies can promote trust as a commercial virtue and also promote particular corporate structures where it is felt that these signal to consumers a greater degree of security.

As noted, credit rating agencies provide one example of a market institution designed to overcome problems caused by information asymmetries.[5] In this context, the chapter by Morrison in Part One is of particular interest because it shows how the incentives of such market institutions can be distorted by regulation. Market signalling mechanisms can also be crowded out by regulation and government guarantees: why does it matter if a bank is trustworthy or has a high level of capital if the regulator exists to look after such things and the government will provide guarantees if things go wrong?

Specific regulation to address specific problems

It would therefore seem that the regulatory response to the financial crash should involve the development of very specific approaches that are designed to deal with well-defined problems. This should help alleviate the regulatory creep that occurs when regulators are given general objectives and unlimited instruments. It also helps those monitoring regulation to hold regulators to account if the regulatory objectives and instruments are well defined. Furthermore, any regulatory response should work with the grain of the market process and not crowd out entrepreneurial initiative that might generate market solutions to the problems that some expect regulators to solve.

There is a precedent for this way of thinking. As Beenstock notes in his chapter in Part One, the early-mid-nineteenth century was a time of chaos in life assurance markets. In 1853 a Select Committee sat and made some recommendations about the future of regulation. To some extent, developments in general company law dealt with the problems and there was little urgency to implement the Select Committee's report. In 1870, however, the Life Insurance Companies Act was passed, which provided very simple remedies to the earlier perceived problems. Information had

---

5   Information asymmetries are a well-defined problem in financial markets – see the seminal paper by Akerlof (1970). Stiglitz was one of the three joint winners of the Nobel Prize, with Akerlof, for work in this field.

to be published to the market by life insurance companies[6] and new legal procedures were developed to handle insolvency.[7] The market operated more or less freely within this framework. Indeed, companies battled with each other to demonstrate that they were the most prudent.

Of course, this was in the days before any state-sponsored insurance schemes, so prudence was a strong commercial selling point for any financial institution. Nevertheless, the general principle is important. Rather than developing more and more detailed and onerous regulation which undermines market incentives, there might be some very simple adjustments to primary law and some very simple regulatory actions that can be taken in order to strengthen market vigilance. After all, millions of consumers monitoring the market – especially as wholesale consumers may have billions of pounds at stake – will always be more effective than 2,000 regulators at the FSA.

So, what are the possible problems that we would like regulation to address? The main ones are perhaps as follows: the systemic risk to the payments system, and the financial system more widely, that arises from the failure of an individual bank; the distorted incentives to banks' customers who are aware that they are protected by deposit insurance; information asymmetries between banks and their counterparties (these run in both directions – for example, they include the non-declaration of information on loan application forms); and the incentives to banks' managers and shareholders caused by bonus systems and limited liability, which reinforce each other. In most cases, existing government regulation either creates or exacerbates these problems. Although we will assume away most government regulation and start with a clean sheet of paper, we will not assume that the deposit insurance scheme is wound up.

The remainder of this chapter looks at the policy ideas that are

---

6   The information was lodged with the Board of Trade but the Board could take no action other than publish correspondence.

7   There was an additional requirement, more controversial, for a company to put down a deposit if it was to enter the market.

implicit or explicit from the chapters in Part One of the book, before summarising the more detailed proposals in Part Two.

Lessons from Part One

Many of the lessons from Part One are general or are not directly related to the new paradigm for bank regulation which is surely necessary. The importance of avoiding monetary booms has been emphasised by Greenwood; Congdon emphasised the crucial role that the central bank should play in managing a crisis. Myddelton called for the repeal of mark-to-market accounting rules, which both make a crisis more likely and make its management more difficult. Morrison warned against the regulation of credit rating agencies that has been proposed. Llewellyn shows how banks can react to their mistakes and, while not ruling out more regulation in certain respects, believes that market correction is all-important. Gregg argues that there needs to be a renewal of virtue within financial markets, something which can, in fact, be crowded out by regulation. These are important contributions to the debate on the future of regulation and the management of crises, even though they do not, perhaps with the exception of Myddelton, actually propose new regulatory approaches.

Butler, though, finds a direct lesson for policymakers. The most obvious lesson is that legislation to achieve one objective can have serious unforeseen effects elsewhere in the economy. The anti-discrimination legislation of the US government increased the risks of the banking system and the implicit guarantees on Fannie Mae and Freddie Mac reduced the incentives of investors to monitor its activities. It would seem difficult to argue that Fannie Mae and Freddie Mac should continue to have a place in the US mortgage market. If the government is going to help the poor obtain better housing conditions at all, this is clearly not best done by distorting the activities of the financial system.

The other chapters in Part One mainly related to international capital regulation. Such regulation reduced incentives to monitor while making more uniform the risk management techniques that were used in banks throughout the world. When those risk management techniques failed, they failed for all banks at the same time. When thinking about the future of international capital regulation, we should begin by asking why it is necessary. The Basel agreement originated because of the concern that differences in regulatory standards would lead to some banks having a competitive advantage over others: if banks supervised in one country were allowed to hold less capital than those supervised in another, then they might be able to offer cheaper loans and obtain more business. A riskier bank should also, however, find it more expensive to obtain funding – including deposit funding – thus cancelling out its advantage. If a bank's domestic government provides implicit or explicit guarantees that make this funding cheaper and these guarantees are trade-distorting then these should perhaps be dealt with through the usual channels that deal with trade-distorting subsidies.

Perhaps international capital regulation is an experiment that has failed. A simple system is bound to be arbitrary, and a complex system will just provide banks with strong incentives to make their operations more complex. Perhaps the most that can be asked is that all banks should publish detailed information to the market. Market analysts are highly sophisticated. If they have made major mistakes in the recent past, one has to ask why. Perhaps the reason is that regulators have assured market participants that capital adequacy has been looked after and the key relationships of those who provide accounting and financial information within a bank have come to be with the regulator and not with market participants. In turn, as Beenstock argues, it is possible that this combination has hindered the process by which information about bank exposure is presented to the market and analysed. Once again, it is worth making the point that millions of market participants who have billions of pounds at stake are likely to be more effective monitors than a few regulators.

New approaches to UK bank regulation

The above discussion mainly relates to general and international considerations. The other authors in Part Two propose specific principles for UK policymakers. They accept the lessons of Austrian economics and public choice economics that regulation should be aimed at very particular weaknesses in the market and that competition should not be inhibited. The particular reason why banks may need to be regulated differently from other firms is that their failure can be systemic because of their impact on the payments system.

Geoffrey Wood proposes that smaller institutions should have their capital *monitored* by the regulators. The minimum level of capital does not necessarily have to be regulated: it merely has to be clear that, if capital falls below a predefined level, the bank will be taken from its shareholders and run by an agency of the government so that, in due course, the bank or its constituent parts can be sold back to the private sector. It should be noted that such a sale might happen quickly because the bank would still have a positive net worth when it was taken from its existing management: the bank may simply need a capital boost. There is no need to take any regulatory action to reduce the risk of failure of smaller banks. Liquidity problems should be dealt with through the lender-of-last-resort facility. If the bank went below the capital limit set by the regulator and was managed by the government for a while before being sold or wound down, the losses would be wholly borne by the shareholders – though debt capital holders would provide an additional cushion. The point of the regime is to change the management of the bank before it has a negative economic value or becomes a burden on taxpayers or the deposit insurance arrangements.

It may be difficult to manage larger banks within such a regime. Again, Wood stresses the importance of the lender-of-last-resort facility when there is a general shortage of liquidity. But he also argues that larger institutions should have higher capital requirements as the external costs of failure are that much greater than for smaller banks. Furthermore, the regulator should have a plan for failure, which is likely to involve briefly managing and then selling off the bank in its component parts.

Thus, in short, we do not need extensive regulation. We need, argues Wood, simple, thoughtful and incisive regulation.

John Kay reinforces these points. There could be mutual compatibility between his proposals and those of Geoffrey Wood but the framework John Kay sets out is slightly different. Kay suggests that we must ensure that depositors and the payments system are protected. This will involve some regulation of deposit-taking institutions. This regulation can be relatively simple, however, given that deposit-taking is a straightforward activity. Then, argues Kay, legislation has to be passed to ensure that the creditors of the deposit-taking part of the institution, together with any deposit insurance schemes, are senior to other creditors in the event of the failure of a conglomerate bank. This has two advantages. First, it would improve incentives for monitoring by the creditors of and investors in what Kay describes as the 'casino' part of the bank. Second, it would ensure that the failure of the casino part would not bring down the payments system or harm depositors.

Llewellyn's discussion is more general. His key recommendation, however, is for a strengthening of market discipline in two ways. First, by government and regulators making it clear that providers of capital will lose their investment in the event of a failure of a bank. Second, Llewellyn emphasises the need for banks to publish information to the market, thus taking a similar position to that of Beenstock. Once again, he has no general confidence in the power of discretionary regulation to achieve more perfect market outcomes but provides an analysis of how particular and limited regulation can help ensure that risk-taking by banks is more limited and better monitored by the market.

Complementary policy changes

At this stage, two further points should be noted. In many ways government policy exacerbated the crash. This has been discussed above.

But two adverse impacts of government policy on risk management in financial markets are rarely mentioned. Government policy, across the Western world, has provided strong incentives for companies to gear their balance sheets and become more risky. This arises as a result of the way in which different forms of investment are taxed. Almost without exception, when a company raises capital by issuing equity, its tax burden is considerably higher than when it raises capital by selling bonds. A UK pension fund, for example, will pay tax at the corporation tax rate of 28 per cent on the return on equity if it holds (say) Royal Bank of Scotland shares. If it holds bond instruments it will have a zero tax rate. The removal of tax credits on dividends in the July 1997 budget exacerbated an already problematic situation. This feature of tax systems leads to incentives for firms to gear their balance sheets and become more risky. It also leads to incentives for institutional investors to hold more credit-related instruments, reducing their yields. Finally, it penalises preference share capital to the point at which such instruments tend to be issued only for the purpose of satisfying certain regulatory objectives: in the past, preference shares have been a useful buffer in the banking system because default on a preference share need not bring a bank into liquidation.

Second, in the UK in particular, various regulatory and other aspects of government policy have encouraged pension funds and insurance companies to hold more bond instruments. Again, this leads, at least indirectly, to more gearing of corporate balance sheets of financial and other companies, thus increasing the risk of failure.

These issues should be addressed. It is perverse for governments to take action that increases risk in the financial system when there is no economic justification for the policy in the first place. The fiscal cost of removing tax discrimination against equity investments may be considerable. It is surely a more urgent priority, however, than the proposed EU crackdown on tax havens.

Conclusion

Our authors' proposals for regulation share characteristics with the changes to company law in the nineteenth century. Serious problems in financial markets at that time were not met with heavy-handed regulation but with incisive primary legislation which applied to insurance companies, banks and the corporate sector more generally. This legislation maintained a liberal market while addressing the particular economic problems that we know can beset specific types of company, particularly in the financial sector. Moreover, these legislative responses in the nineteenth century were enduring, lasting for 100 years or more, and did not spawn millions of paragraphs of secondary legislation and accompanying regulations. These approaches were adopted in the nineteenth century after many years of thoughtful consideration, including by select committees of Parliament.

In the wake of the financial crash, the choice before us is really quite simple. We can accept the implausible hypothesis that giving broad general powers of regulatory oversight to a government bureau will necessarily improve market outcomes. Alternatively, we can use thoughtful economic analysis to identify specific problems in financial markets and resolve those with a simple and targeted legislative framework. It is evident that giving wide discretionary powers to statutory regulatory bodies has not prevented financial market collapse. Indeed, it could be argued that these bodies have used their discretionary powers arbitrarily and in ways that have hindered rather than helped the development of self-correcting processes within markets. It is perhaps time to restore the primacy of market discipline – backed up, if necessary, by specific legislation targeted at well-understood weaknesses.

References

Akerlof, G. A. (1970), 'The market for lemons: quality uncertainty and the market mechanism', *Quarterly Journal of Economics*, 84(3): 488–500.

De Soto. J. H. (2008), *The Austrian School: Market Order and Entrepreneurial Creativity*, Cheltenham: Edward Elgar.

Financial Services Authority (2008), 'The supervision of Northern Rock: a lessons learned review', Report of the FSA Internal Audit Division, London: FSA.

Tullock, G. (2006), *The Vote Motive*, Hobart Paperback 33, London: Institute of Economic Affairs.

15 THOUGHTFUL REGULATION
Geoffrey Wood[1]

Introduction

The regulation of banks has failed. It must be tougher. It will be more expensive. Everyone is agreed on these propositions. Such universal agreement is unusual, and is actually easily explained. The first two statements have many possible meanings, and the third is an inevitable part of any government's response to a problem – more must be spent.

My aim is to set out what I think should be meant by the first two remarks, and to set out an outline of the kind of regulation to which that leads. First, though, what do I mean by a bank? It is a business that takes retail and wholesale deposits and makes loans; it contributes by its loans to the money stock, and is part of the payments system. Investment banks, whether of the traditional advisory sort or the modern type that keeps loans on its own books, are for the purposes of this discussion set aside, with the remark only that when they fail it must be orderly, with due regard for the numerous types of contract and counterparty that they have. When a bank that does both kinds of business fails, the traditional banking part should be handled as described below, and the investment banking part closed in an orderly manner, and any remaining value used to protect the 'traditional banking' part.

The regulation of all banks

Why are traditional banks regulated? All firms are regulated, but banks

1   I am indebted to Rae Balbach for insightful comments on a draft.

are regulated in a way different from any non-financial firm. There is regulation of how much capital they have, and regular testing to see whether it is adequate to withstand a range of possible shocks. What is the point of this? It is undoubtedly troublesome if a bank fails; there is disruption to the businesses and lives of its customers in ways and to an extent that are not true of the failure of most kinds of firm. This does not, however, require extensive regulation, but rather a legal framework so that a bank can 'fail' while continuing to operate. That is to say, as in the USA, it should be possible to take a bank away from its shareholders and management while it is still solvent, and keep it running so that all who transact with it can continue doing so. The bank can then be sold on, in an orderly way, in whole or in parts, to buyers who will keep it running and restore it to financial health. The proceeds from the sale can be used to settle the bank's debts, and anything left should go to the shareholders.

This can be the procedure for many banks within the financial system and, for banks for which that can be done, the choice of capital ratio could be left to the management of the institutions concerned; the bank would simply be told that if it went below some fairly arbitrary capital level set by the regulator then the bank would be taken over in the way described above. Such a facility exists in the USA, has been proposed in the UK by the Treasury Select Committee of the House of Commons, and is now being advanced in a bill currently going through Parliament. With that in place, why is any regulation different from that of non-financial firms necessary?

The answer to that question is in two parts. First, if banks are to be capable of being closed while still solvent, their capital must be monitored, and not just by their management – for in distress there would be, at the least, a desire to be optimistic. That is why there needs to be some capital regulation, or at least oversight, of all banks. But this regulation does not have to be onerous, expensive or overly complex. Second, some banks are so big that taking them over and running them would present enormous problems. It is preferable that such large banks do not fail and these banks need extra attention in the regulatory regime.

The regulation of larger banks

In the remainder of this chapter I focus on that second reason for regulation, on the grounds that smaller banks are adequately dealt with by monitoring and prompt closure when necessary.[2] How should 'large' banks be regulated?

A digression on liquidity is necessary at this point, for a liquidity shortage can quickly turn into a capital shortage if it forces asset sales at distressed prices. Banks must hold assets that can be readily turned into cash at the central bank. These assets must of course include government paper, but they can extend beyond that, for in a time of general shortage of liquidity the central bank should accept a wide range of securities in exchange for cash. In doing so the central bank would be following the precedent set by the Bank of England, to such stabilising effect, in the nineteenth century, when it started to implement the concept of lender of last resort. Of course, that action is intended to relieve only a general shortage of liquidity; if an institution cannot get liquidity from financial markets when these markets are not paralysed by panic then that is an institution which has run out of generally acceptable collateral, will start undertaking distress sales, and will soon collapse into the insolvency regime. These points on liquidity apply to small and to large banks alike.

And that brings us back to banks that are too big for the special insolvency regime – not 'too big to fail' in the sense often used in the academic banking literature, but so big that managing an orderly 'failure' in the sense in which small banks can fail in an orderly fashion would be hard. Such banks raise two problems. The first is how to diminish their risks of failure, and the second is what to do about them in the long term.

Such large banks should require higher capital ratios than small banks. This is counter-intuitive at first glance, because size usually brings diversification, and diversification brings stability. But that is to neglect the problems caused by the failure of such institutions. Given that the problems with large banks arise when they fail, the capital

---

2   They would therefore be essentially unregulated apart from the monitoring of their capital.

requirement for such banks must be modelled under extreme assumptions. Extreme outcomes do sometimes occur and regulators cannot be as sanguine as they can be for banks that can be taken over in the way described above. Hence, capital ratios should be high. What is 'high'? A way of thinking about this would be to look back and see what capital ratios were required over a period of years, good and bad, for such banks to have the same return on equity as other types of large firms in industries where competition, in the sense of freedom of entry and exit, prevailed. That would be a good starting point.

But it is not a good finishing point. The reason is that it neglects incentives. There is much concern about the bonuses bankers have received. This concern is largely regarding their size, and therefore manages to miss not one point but several.

The first point is that there is nothing wrong with bonuses, but they must be framed so as to ensure that in a business where continuity is important, they reward not the signing of a deal but its successful conclusion. Second, there should be attention to incentive structures from top to bottom of the firm, and these structures should, as at the top, encourage efforts to maintain profits rather than simply reward individual deals. Transactions-oriented reward structures should be eschewed. An illustration of the importance of this is given by the much more rapid deterioration of the mortgage books of those firms which relied on independent financial advisers for mortgage business rather than getting it through their own staff dealing, either online or in person, with the mortgagee. Bonuses should be paid on the final completion of a deal, not on its successful initiation. That would have an additional benefit – it would ensure that deals were monitored throughout their life, and perhaps even encourage banks to keep a small stake in every transaction they initiated. At the least, they would not be able to pursue a policy of 'originate and forget'. Third, management should be required to hold shares in their company. This is not foolproof – there was extensive such holding of Lehman's shares – but it should help to ensure caution, especially if the shares could not be sold until some years (five is a nice round number) after retirement or otherwise leaving the firm.[3] Who imposes these rules is considered immediately below.

Now we come to the firms' owners, the shareholders. In the UK, bank shareholders appear sometimes to be a rather strange group. They are strange in that they sometimes behave differently with regard to the banks they own than they do with regard to other types of firm they own. With banks, they can be passive, accepting what the management does to them. With other firms they are much more active in their monitoring. This does not happen all the time – but the takeover by RBS of a foreign bank at the very peak of an asset price boom is a truly striking example of shareholder passivity. It might be helpful if shareholders became at least as active with banks as they are with their other investments.[4] If they do not do so, and fail to pay adequate attention to the incentive structures in the firms they own, should regulators do it for them? That would be extraordinarily intrusive upon rights of ownership; and worse, it might not be effective. The same incentive structure is unlikely to be appropriate across all banks; the managers and owners have information about their own firms that no outsider can possibly have, and they are therefore far and away the best able to devise a sensible incentive structure. There can be no harm in regulators setting out what they see as a set of principles to guide incentive structures, but these should be for discussion, comment and, if shareholders wish, rejection. The consequences of getting it wrong fall primarily on them.

But with all that done, there is yet more. Regulators should prepare for failure. They should do that because it is almost certain that something will go wrong at some time, and because the consequence of lack of preparedness when Northern Rock got into difficulties was a nearly disastrous bank run. This preparation should have two parts. The regulators should regularly plan what they are going to do in the event of a big bank needing help, and, because each bank will be somewhat

---

3   Death would also trigger the right to sell.
4   One has to say 'might' because the one active major shareholder in a bank targeted very aggressively HSBC, a bank that seemed to be in better shape than most.

different, there should be a plan for every bank, and these plans should be regularly updated. The regulators should also plan, and announce that they have planned, to sell off in parts, not as a whole, any big bank that they have to take over. This would have three benefits. It would reduce competition problems arising from the existence of large banks capable perhaps of setting up barriers to entry. While this may not be a problem worldwide, it will surely become so in the UK given the Lloyds Bank takeover of HBOS; after all, competition rules had to be formally waived to allow it to be approved in principle by regulators. Second, it would further encourage management to be cautious. And perhaps most importantly it would, if carried out, get rid of one of these troublesome big banks, and give us a few more that would not be 'too big to fail easily'.

In summary, thoughtful regulation would not involve more detailed micromanagement of banks. It would involve careful thought about regulatory structures and incentives. Get these even roughly right, and the details will sort themselves out.

16 THE FUTURE OF FINANCIAL SERVICES REGULATION

John Kay

There is almost universal agreement that 'more effective regulation' must be the price of the bank bailouts. There is, however, almost no specificity about what that 'more effective regulation' might do. Or what it might have done. What measures were not in place, but might in future be in place, that would have prevented the collapse of Northern Rock and Bradford & Bingley, or the tribulations of HBOS? Would such regulation have blocked the hubristic takeover of ABN Amro by Royal Bank of Scotland? What regulatory scrutiny was there, or should there be, of Barclays' takeover of the US operations of the failed Lehman Bros? In every one of these cases, the issues are not technical ones of capital adequacy or of liquidity ratios, but fundamental questions of business strategy. Is that what future regulation of financial services is to be about?

The need for bank regulation is not open to question. Banks have demonstrated – if fresh demonstration were necessary – that they have the power to impose losses on millions of entirely innocent and prudent savers and businesses and the capacity to endanger the growth and stability of the global economy. These consequences cannot be eliminated, but much can be done to ameliorate them. And even if that were not true, laissez-faire is not a conceivable political option.

The difficulties of discretionary regulation

But effective regulation of an industry led by powerful figures and populated by traders driven by ego and greed is difficult. All regulation is fraught with unintended consequences. And this is certainly true of financial regulation. The early effects of risk-weighted capital require-ments for banks involved stimulating the development of the securitisa-tion market, which reduced the risk weighting attached to substantially similar transactions. The explosion of securitisation is at the root of many of today's problems.

Experience of regulation across other industries shows that it works best when carefully directed to specific evils. The paradigm case is the regulation of airlines. Regulation to secure airline safety is obviously necessary. But regulatory creep extended the scope of supervision to almost all airline activities, controlling fares and routes: such regula-tion ultimately served no interest other than that of established airlines, and perhaps not even those. Airline regulation is now more appropri-ately targeted. We have today both a competitive aviation industry and the confidence we need that the planes that fly over central London are unlikely to cause us injury.

Another general lesson of regulation is that structural remedies should generally be preferred to behavioural ones. It is better to prevent monopolies from coming into being than to control their activities: better to separate functions than to supervise the relations between different parts of the same firm.

The casino and the utility

The Great Depression in the United States led to the establishment of the Securities and Exchange Commission. The Glass-Steagall Act, which recognised how conflicts of interest had worked to the disadvantage of small customers, required the separation of investment and retail banking. But over time, banks turned into financial conglomerates.

Such conglomerate banks contain large hedge funds – assemblies of speculative trading positions. But if a hedge fund makes losses of 5 per cent of its assets, it has a bad year: if too many unhappy investors seek to liquidate their positions quickly, it can suspend redemptions. Many hedge funds have recently had one or both experiences. But if a bank loses 5 per cent of its assets, or needs to suspend redemptions, it is bust. That is, roughly speaking, what has happened.

The modern financial services industry is a casino attached to a utility. The utility is the payments system, which enables individuals and non-financial companies to manage their daily affairs. The utility allows them to borrow and lend for their routine activities, and allocates finance in line with the fundamental value of business activities. In the casino, traders make profits from arbitrage and short-term price movements. The users of the utility look to fundamental values. The occupants of the casino are preoccupied with the mind of the market.

Modest levels of speculative activity may improve the operation of the utility. By exploiting arbitrage opportunities, they can bring the mind of the market back in line with fundamental values. But as trading levels increase, the mind of the market, determined by the power of conventional thinking, becomes itself the main influence on prices.

Where there has been abuse, there will be regulation. Looking forward, the primary objective of the regulation of financial services should be that the casino should never again jeopardise the utility. Many people seem to think that the best method of achieving this is close supervision of the casino. This notion is misconceived.

The impossibility and undesirability of regulating the casino

There needs to be realism about what regulation can achieve. It is undesirable, and potentially costly in very many different ways, for government to recognise obligations it cannot in practice discharge. Regulators cannot be expected to decide which financial innovations are necessary and which not. Nor can they act systematically to restrict unsound business strategies.

The junior officials of a public agency do not have the capability, or the authority, to advise bankers paid multimillion-pound salaries and bonuses against what, with the benefit of hindsight, appear to be errors in the direction of their business. It is improbable that they could have this capability or authority – after all, the boards of these institutions did not. Nor should we assume that, if regulators did have such capacity, they could effectively exercise it in a world in which the financial services industry is the most powerful political lobby in the country and the threat of judicial review hangs over every regulatory action.

The practical result of such 'more effective' regulation – which is now inevitable – will be more international meetings, and institutions, and an expansion of the staff of regulatory agencies and of the compliance departments of financial services businesses. The additional rules that will be introduced as a consequence will be irrelevant to the next bubble, as the Basel I and II capital requirements imposed on banks – the subject of so much debate over the last two decades – were irrelevant in the credit bubble.

The protection of retail customers

The primary object of regulation should not be to ensure good practice in financial services businesses, but to protect retail customers. Its purpose should be consumer protection directed, not at removing information asymmetry, but at relieving its consequences. There is no escaping the stark contrast between the size and general profitability of the financial services industry and the poor service it delivers to its retail customers. The best advice that can be given on selecting products is, in most cases, to buy the cheapest and to do as much as possible yourself.

Neither regulation nor markets will ever ensure that ordinary retail investors receive good personalised financial advice. The economics of the business makes such provision impossible. We select clothes and food, furniture and cars, for ourselves from the shelf or the showroom floor because the services of skilled, knowledgeable, impartial intermediaries cost more than we are willing to pay. The cost of high-quality professional services is much greater. Bespoke legal advice is priced out of reach and medical advice accessible only because it is made free. The most that can be expected in retail financial services is the confidence generated by a large supermarket, where you justifiably believe that the store's concern for its reputation means that the products you find will be fit for purpose and good value for money.

Preventing the casino from destroying the utility

We should look for structural solutions to the problems of financial stability – to seek to separate the utility from the casino. The purpose would be to restore the 'narrow banking'[1] that once existed – the business of facilitating the payment system, taking small deposits, and lending to meet the day-to-day needs of consumers and small and medium-sized businesses. Narrow banking is an activity that requires little flair and imagination, rather the conscientious completion of millions of transactions a day with minimal error. While technology and financial innovation have changed the processes by which narrow banking is provided, the customer needs that are served have changed very little.

Financial conglomerates are, as Senators Glass and Steagall recognised, a bad idea. They are a bad idea for their shareholders, victims of recurrent tension between investment and retail bankers within a single corporate organisation; a bad idea for customers, because conglomerates are riddled with conflicts of interest; and a bad idea for taxpayers, who have to pick up the bills when traders driven by avarice and hubris have gambled with retail customers' savings.

A new Glass-Steagall Act would probably not work, as the old Glass-Steagall ultimately did not work. For the moment the collapse of the credit bubble has actually strengthened the role of conglomerates, because the scale of resources of retail banks, with large deposit bases, exceeds that of stand-alone investment banks. Although diversified financial conglomerates do not serve the interests of those who work for them, own their shares or use their services, they do serve the interests of the greedy and ambitious men who run them, and their aspirations will

---

1   Narrow banking can have several different interpretations. I am using the term here in a general way.

challenge and find ways round any such restrictions in the future as they have done in the past.

Instead, structural rules should firewall the utility from the casino, by giving absolute priority to retail depositors (or the institutions that protect retail depositors) in the event of the failure of a deposit-taking institution. The players at the casino can then make such rules (or none) to govern their own activities as they think appropriate. Those who contract with the casino – on the whole sophisticated players in the financial system – would be aware of the risks of their contractual claims being subordinated to those of the utility part of a conglomerate bank. The primary object of regulation should not be to ensure good practice in financial services businesses, but to protect the non-financial customers of financial institutions. There is a fundamental public interest in keeping crooks out of wholesale financial markets; but that is as far as public involvement need, or should, go. And public authorities should feel no obligation to facilitate the smooth functioning of markets, especially when there is no evident public benefit from the market having come into existence in the first place. It is time for less regulation of financial services, not more.

17 THE GLOBAL FINANCIAL CRISIS: INCENTIVE STRUCTURES AND IMPLICATIONS FOR REGULATION

David T. Llewellyn

In my chapter in Part One, I considered the role of financial innovation (and credit-risk shifting instruments in particular) as a significant factor in the global financial crisis. This chapter considers two further issues: the role of incentive structures in the crisis, and some implications with respect to regulation, regulatory strategy and supervision within a holistic regulatory regime.

Causes of the crisis: incentive structures

The chapter in Part 1 outlined some of the incentive implications inherent in the new banking models that emerged as a result of financial innovation. These focused on adverse selection and moral hazard. There are several other ways in which perverse incentive structures have contributed to the current crisis. Reward structures within banks are often based on the volume of business undertaken; the extent to which the risk characteristics of decisions are or are not incorporated into management reward structures; the nature of internal control systems within banks; internal monitoring of the decision-making of loan officers; the nature of profit-sharing schemes and the extent to which decision-makers also share in losses, and so on. Reward systems based on short-term profits can be hazardous as they are prone to induce managers to pay less attention to the longer-term risk characteristics of their decisions. High staff turnover, and the speed with which officers are moved within the bank, may also create incentives for excessive risk-taking. A similar effect can arise through the herd behaviour that is not uncommon in banking. The incentive structures favouring 'short-termism' are epitomised in the now infamous statement of the chairman of Citi (Chuck Prince): 'As long as the music is playing, you've got to get up and dance. We're still dancing.' This problem has been noted by several academics. Buiter (2008) suggests: 'one of the key drivers of the excesses of the most recent (and earlier) financial booms has been the myopic and asymmetric reward structure in many financial institutions'. Mizen (2008) identifies several hazardous incentives structures within the 'originate to distribute' banking model characterised by the securitisation of bank lending. He also highlights the incentives of rating agencies, which may be subject to conflicts of interest as they often advise on how to structure instruments in order to receive a favourable rating.

Overall, there is evidence that reward structures within banks can produce a bias towards excessive risk-taking. In particular, UBS (2008) has identified systemic deficiencies in its own compensation policy as a contributory factor in the substantial write-downs it has suffered. Bank of England governor Mervyn King, in oral evidence to the House of Commons Treasury Select Committee in April 2008, argued that 'banks themselves have come to realise, in the recent crisis, that they are paying the price themselves for having designed compensation packages which provide incentives that are not, in the long run, in the interests of the banks themselves'.

Corporate governance arrangements need to provide for effective monitoring and supervision of the risk-taking profile of banks. These arrangements need to provide for *inter alia* a management structure with clear lines of accountability; independent non-executive directors of the board; independent audit committees; transparent ownership structures; internal structures that enable the risk profile of the firm to be clearly transparent and managed; and the creation and monitoring of risk analysis and management systems.

Regulation is an important, but only one, component of a regime designed to achieve the objectives of systemic stability and the safety and soundness of financial institutions (Llewellyn, 2001). Giving too much emphasis to regulation per se carries the danger that the importance of the other components are downplayed, or even marginalised. There is always a danger that the regulation component, if pressed too far, will blunt other mechanisms and in the process compromise the overall impact of the regime. For instance, the more emphasis that is given to detailed, extensive and prescriptive rules, the weaker might be the role of incentive structures, market discipline and corporate governance arrangements within financial firms. Similarly, an excessive focus on detailed and prescriptive rules may weaken corporate governance mechanisms within financial firms, and may blunt the incentive of others to monitor and control the behaviour of banks. The way intervention is conducted in the event of bank distress (e.g. whether forbearance is practised) may also have adverse incentive effects on the behaviour of banks and the willingness of markets to monitor and control banks' risk-taking.

It would be a mistake to rely wholly, or even predominantly, on external regulation and monitoring and supervision by the official sector. The world of banking and finance is too complex and volatile to warrant dependence on a single set of prescriptive rules for prudent behaviour. The central role of incentive structures in particular needs to be constantly emphasised, as there are many reasons why incentive structures within financial firms may not be aligned with regulatory objectives (Llewellyn, 1999).

The central challenge for the regulator in devising a regulatory strategy lies in how the various components in the regime are combined. A critique of current arrangements is that it has been excessively 'rules-based', with insufficient attention to the other components of the regime. The challenge for future regulatory strategy is to optimise the whole regime and in particular to give less emphasis to detailed and prescriptive rules, and more to incentive structures within financial firms, a strengthening of market discipline, more focus on banks' risk analysis and management systems, and a strengthening of corporate governance arrangements within financial firms. The distinction between regulation per se and a focus on incentive structures should not, however, be pressed too far as, to some extent, elements of regulation operate through creating incentives for banks to behave in an appropriate way. The point is that the formal rules component of the regulatory regime is only one element in the incentive structures faced by bank managers. With respect to empirical evidence, on the basis of statistical analysis of over 150 countries, Barth et al. (2006) conclude that 'an approach to bank supervision and regulation that stresses private monitoring tends to boost the operation of banks more effectively than an approach based on direct official oversight and restrictions on banks'.

Incentive structures in the regulatory regime

Incentive structures and moral hazards faced by decision-makers (bank owners and managers, lenders to banks, borrowers and regulators) are major parts of the regulatory regime. The overall issue is twofold. There need to be internal incentives for management to behave in appropriate ways, and the regulator has a role in ensuring internal incentives are compatible with regulatory objectives. A central role for regulation and supervision is to create appropriate incentives within regulated firms so that the incentives faced by decision-makers are consistent with the soundness of financial institutions and financial stability.

At the same time, regulation needs to avoid the danger of blunting the incentives of other agents (for example, rating agencies, depositors, shareholders, debt-holders) that have a disciplining role with banks. The position has been put well by Schinasi et al. (1999): 'Policy makers are therefore faced with the difficult challenge of balancing efforts to manage systemic risk against efforts to ensure that market participants bear the costs of imprudent risk taking and have incentives to behave prudently.' They argue that banks have complex incentive structures. There are internal incentives that motivate key decision-makers involved with risk; corporate governance mechanisms (such as accountability to shareholders); an external market in corporate control; market disciplines which may affect the cost of capital and deposits; and accountability to bank supervisors. The presence of regulation and official supervision overlays the structure of incentives faced by bank decision-makers.

Incentive structures need to be considered at two levels: (1) the impact that regulation and supervision have on incentives within banks, and (2) the incentive properties of reward structures within banks.

How regulators can create perverse incentives

This means that a central consideration for the regulator is the impact its own rules have on regulated firms' incentive structures, whether they might have perverse effects, and what regulation can do to improve incentives. Incentive structures are central to all aspects of regulation because if these are wrong it is unlikely that the other mechanisms in the regime will achieve regulatory objectives. If one form of regulation produces inappropriate incentive structures then other forms of regulation will not be successful. Incentive structures are therefore at the heart of the regulatory process.

In the immediate context of the recent crisis, a particular perversity focused on the way the Basel Capital Accord created incentives for banks to develop the originate-and-distribute model, which, as argued in the chapter in Part One, was a key element in the origin of the crisis. It also created incentives for banks to hold assets off the balance sheet. In effect, regulation created incentives for financial intermediation business to be shifted to unregulated 'shadow banks'. While, on the face of it, this had the appearance of shifting credit risk away from the banks, what appeared to be a credit-risk-shifting strategy helped create a liquidity crisis and then a funding crisis. In the event, credit risk was not shifted as much as was thought and, even when it was shifted, it changed the nature of the risk.

Regulators and the monitoring of incentives

Supervisors need to give consideration to the incentive properties of compensation schemes within banks and the extent to which they are likely to induce imprudent behaviour (see, for instance, Rajan, 2005; Knight, 2004). Remuneration systems that imply limited downside risk but high upside potential for managers, and front-loaded payouts, are likely to create incentives for managers towards excessive risk-taking. The position has been put well by Kodres (2008):

> Unless the governance structure within major financial institutions changes so that both risk and business line managers have equal weight in senior management's eyes, senior managers are unlikely to pay sufficient attention to the risk part of the risk–reward trade-off. Ideally, traders should be rewarded on a risk-adjusted basis and managers on a cyclically adjusted basis.

Reward structures need to become an issue for supervisors. While there is nothing that regulation or supervision can, or should, do to dictate reward structures within firms, the degree of supervisory intervention and attention could be calibrated on the basis of the incentive structures created by institutions' remuneration structures. There are several possible ways this could be done. For example, regulators could increase the degree of supervision of a bank if its internal reward structures are judged to be biased towards excessive risk-taking. This could include applying specific regulatory requirements if the reward structures were deemed to increase risk. Regulators could also give warnings to banks that they have concerns about incentive structures. In practice, however, there are limits to what supervisors can do in this area without imposing inappropriate interventionist inroads into the reward structure of banks. Nevertheless, given that supervisors have the responsibility of considering the risk characteristics of bank strategies, and their internal models, supervisors do have power to consider the implications of remuneration structures in the way they supervise banks. The position has been put well by the chief executive of the FSA:

From the regulatory point of view, it is not our role to dictate the quantum of individual remuneration, that is for the market, but we do need to consider the implications of remuneration structures when judging the overall risk of individual institutions. We will do this with increased intensity. (Sants, 2008)

This statement suggests that at least one regulatory agency plans to take on board the risk implications of remuneration packages of bank officers and the incentive structures they create.

Incentives and intervention

Incentive arrangements also apply to supervisory authorities, and most especially with regard to when and how to intervene in the event of bank distress. The credible threat of closure of an insolvent or, under a Structured Early Intervention and Resolution (SEIR) regime, a near-insolvent bank can impose a powerful discipline on the future behaviour of banks. Such 'creative destruction' has a positive dimension. It is also necessary to define the nature of 'closure'. It does not necessarily mean that, even in the absence of deposit insurance, depositors lose. Nor do bank–customer relationships and information sharing need to be destroyed. Bank closure may simply mean a change in ownership of a bank and the imposition of losses on equity holders. In most countries, 'bank closure' has not meant the destruction of the bank. In many instances, regulatory authorities have brokered a change in ownership of insolvent banks while imposing losses on shareholders. The skill in intervention that leads to the 'closure' of an institution lies in ensuring that what remains of value is maintained.

Intervention arrangements are important not least because they have incentive and moral hazard effects which potentially influence future behaviour by banks and their customers. These arrangements may also have important implications for the total cost of intervention (for example, initial forbearance often has the effect of raising the eventual cost of subsequent intervention), and the distribution of those costs between taxpayers and other agents. Different intervention arrangements also have implications for the future efficiency of the financial system in that, for instance, forbearance may have the effect of sustaining inefficient banks and excess capacity in the banking sector.

The issue focuses on when intervention is to be made. The experience of banking crises in both developed and developing countries indicates that a well-defined strategy for responding to the possible insolvency of financial institutions is needed. An optimal response strategy in the event of bank distress has three key components:

- taking prompt corrective action to address financial problems before they reach critical proportions;
- being prepared to close insolvent financial institutions while nevertheless not destroying what value remains;
- closing unviable institutions, and vigorously monitoring weak and/ or restructured institutions.

A central issue relates to the use of rules versus discretion in the event of bank distress: the extent to which intervention should be circumscribed by clearly defined rules (so that intervention agencies have no discretion about whether, how and when to act), or whether there should always be discretion simply because relevant circumstances cannot be set out in advance. The obvious prima facie advantage for allowing discretion is that it is impossible to foresee all future circumstances and conditions in which a bank might become distressed and close to (or actually) insolvent. It might be judged that it is not always the right policy to close a bank in such circumstances.

There are, however, strong arguments against allowing such discretion and in favour of a rules-based approach to intervention. First, it enhances the credibility of the intervention agency in that market participants, including banks, have a high degree of certainty that action will be taken. Second, allowing discretion may increase the probability of forbearance, which usually leads to higher costs when intervention is finally made. Kane (2000), for instance, argues that officials may forbear because they face different incentives from those of the market: their own welfare, the interests of the agency they represent, political interests, reputation, future employment prospects, etc. Third, a rules-based approach removes the danger of undue political interference in the disciplining of banks and regulated firms. Experience in many countries indicates that supervisory authorities face substantial pressure to delay action and intervention. Fourth, and related to the first, a rules approach to intervention is likely to have a beneficial impact on *ex ante* behaviour of financial firms. By removing any prospect that a hazardous bank might be treated leniently, a rules-based approach enhances the incentives for bank managers to manage their banks prudently so as to reduce the probability of insolvency (Glaessner and Mas, 1995). It also guards against risk-averse supervisors being inclined to delay intervention for fear that action would be interpreted as a supervisory failure.

Put another way, time-inconsistency and credibility problems should be addressed through pre-commitments and graduated responses with the possibility of overrides. Many analysts have advocated various forms of predetermined intervention through a general policy of 'Structured Early Intervention and Resolution' (SEIR). There is a case for a graduated-response approach since, for example, there is no magical capital ratio below which an institution is in danger and above which it is safe. Other things being equal, potential danger gradually increases as the capital ratio declines. This in itself suggests that there should be a graduated series of responses from the regulator as capital diminishes. No single dividing line should trigger action, but there should be a series of such trigger points with the effect of going through any one of them being relatively minor, but the cumulative effect being large. An example of the rules-based approach is to be found in the Prompt Corrective Action (PCA) rules in the USA. These specify graduated intervention by the regulators with predetermined responses triggered by capital thresholds. Several countries have such rules of intervention (Basel Committee, 1999). SEIR strategies can, therefore, act as a powerful incentive for prudent behaviour. The need to maintain the credibility of supervisory agencies also creates a strong case against forbearance.

The role of market discipline

A major component of the regulatory regime relates to the arrangements for market discipline on banks. Regulation can never be an alternative to market discipline. On the contrary, market discipline needs to be reinforced within the regime. In well-developed regimes, the market has incentives to monitor the behaviour of financial firms. The disciplines imposed by the market can be as powerful as any sanctions imposed by official agencies. The disciplining role of the markets (including the interbank market) was weak prior to the recent crisis.

Market discipline works through three channels: prices (of, for instance, the cost of debt and equity), quantities (the willingness of investors to supply resources to a bank) and triggers for official supervisory intention. With respect to the last-mentioned, supervisors need to use market signals as one of their information sources upon which to base any case for intervention. This was evidently not done in the case of Northern Rock (Hamaleinan, 2009).

A paradigm for considering the required conditions for market discipline to work effectively is outlined in Llewellyn (2001 and 2004), and introduces the concept of stakeholder monitors: those who have an incentive to monitor the risk-taking and other strategies of banks. Monitoring is a costly activity, which means that for there to be incentives for stakeholder monitors to undertake it there needs to be a balance between costs and benefits. This in turn implies that stakeholders need to be at risk of loss if monitoring is not conducted. This may be undermined by, for instance, perceptions that particular banks are regarded as being 'too big to fail', generous deposit protection arrangements, policies (or perceived policies) of forbearance, and bailouts of one sort or another. If stakeholders believe they will not lose in the event of a bank's hazardous behaviour, they have no incentive to engage in costly monitoring. On the contrary, if they gain when risky behaviour is profitable but believe they will not lose in the event of failure, the perceived asymmetric reward structure is a clear disincentive for monitors to seek to limit the risk-taking of banks.

This implies that regulatory strategy should focus on what can be done to lower the costs of monitoring (by, for instance, requiring more, relevant and comparable information disclosure by banks), and increasing the benefits (by, for instance, limiting the perception that stakeholders will not lose if they fail to limit banks' risk-taking). Adequate information and disclosure requirements are at the centre of a regime to enhance the potential for market discipline to work. Such information disclosure needs to relate to all aspects of a bank's risk profile, including, for instance, the exposure to off-balance-sheet vehicles, the nature of a bank's total risk exposure, and the quality of collateral. There also needs to be greater harmonisation of reporting standards of off-balance-sheet vehicles.

Market discipline works effectively only on the basis of full and accurate information disclosure and transparency. Good-quality, timely and relevant information needs to be available to all market participants and regulators so that asset quality, creditworthiness and the condition of financial institutions can be adequately assessed. The central importance of transparency is emphasised in Borio and Tsatsaronis (2004 and 2006). In a study of the conduct of regulation in over 150 countries, Barth et al. (2006) conclude: '... regulation that requires informational transparency and that strengthens the ability and incentives of the private sector to monitor banks tends to promote sound banking'.

A major factor behind the current financial market turmoil was uncertainty regarding which institutions were holding what risks as a result of issuing and trading credit derivatives. It was largely the lack of transparency in the pricing of structured credit instruments that lay at the bottom of the current financial crisis. The problem was focused on a range of opaque financial instruments being traded by opaque financial vehicles. The experience of the financial crisis suggests regulatory and supervisory intervention in several areas, and especially the need for more transparency of financial instruments (particularly with respect to their full risk characteristics), and greater transparency regarding financial institutions' use of credit and other derivatives so that the risk profile of institutions is easier to detect.

Conclusion

Effective regulation and supervision of banks and financial institutions has the potential to make a significant contribution to the stability and robustness of a financial system. There are, however, limits to what regulation and supervision can achieve in practice. Although regulation is an important part of the regulatory regime, it is only one part, and the other components are equally important. In the final analysis, there is no viable alternative to placing the main responsibility for risk management and general compliance on the shoulders of the management of financial institutions. Management must not be able to hide behind the cloak of regulation or pretend that, if regulation and supervisory arrangements are in place, this absolves them from their own responsibility. Nothing should ever be seen as taking away the responsibility for supervision of financial firms from shareholders, managers and the markets.

The objective is to optimise the outcome of a regulatory strategy in terms of mixing the components of the regime, bearing in mind that some aspects of the regime can militate against the effectiveness of other parts. The emphasis is on the combination of mechanisms rather than alternative approaches to achieving the objectives. Those devising regulatory strategy must pay careful attention to how various components are combined, and how the various instruments available to the regulator (rules, principles, guidelines, mandatory disclosure requirements, authorisation, supervision, intervention, sanctions, redress, etc.) are to be used.

References

Barth, J., G. Caprio and R. Levine (2006), *Rethinking Bank Regulation: Till Angels Govern*, Cambridge: Cambridge University Press.

Basel Committee (1999), 'A new capital adequacy framework', Consultative Paper, Basel: Basel Committee on Banking Supervision, BIS, June.

Borio, C. and K. Tsatsaronis (2004), 'Accounting and prudential regulation: from uncomfortable bedfellows to perfect partners?', *Journal of Financial Stability*, September.

Borio, C. and K. Tsatsaronis (2006), 'Risk in financial reporting: status and suggested future directions', BIS Working Papers no. 213, August.

Buiter, W. (2008), 'Lessons from Northern Rock: how to handle failure', in A. Felton and C. Reinhart (eds), *The First Global Financial Crisis of the 21st Century*, London: CEPR.

Glaessner, T. and I. Mas (1995), 'Incentives and the resolution of bank distress', *World Bank Research Observer*, 10(1): 53–73.

Hamaleinan, P. (2009), 'Fallout from the credit squeeze and Northern Rock crises: incentives, transparency and the role of market discipline', in F. Bruni and D. Llewellyn (eds), *The Northern Rock Crisis*, Vienna: SUERF.

Kane, E. (2000), 'Dynamic inconsistency of capital forbearance: long run vs short run effects of too-big-to-fail policymaking', Paper presented to IMF Central Banking Conference, Washington, DC, June.

Knight, M. (2004), 'Markets and institutions: managing the evolving financial risk', 25th SUERF Colloquium, Bank for International Settlements, Basel, October.

Kodres, L. (2008), 'A crisis of confidence and a lot more', *Finance and Development*, June, pp. 8–13.

Llewellyn, D. T. (1999), *The Economic Rationale of Financial Regulation and Supervision*, FSA Occasional Paper no. 1, London: Financial Services Authority.

Llewellyn, D. T. (2001), 'A regulatory regime for financial stability', in G. Kaufman (ed.), *Bank Fragility and Regulation: Evidence from Different Countries*, Amsterdam: JAI.

Llewellyn, D. T. (2004), 'Inside the black box of market discipline', in C. Borio, W. Hunter, G. Kaufman and K. Tsatsaronis (eds), *Market Discipline across Countries and Industries*, MIT Press.

Mizen, P. (2008), 'The credit crunch of 2007–2008: a discussion of the background, market reactions and policy responses', Federal Reserve Bank of St Louis, *Review*, September.

Rajan, R. G. (2005), 'Has financial development made the world riskier', Washington, DC: International Monetary Fund, August.

Sants, H. (2008), Speech at the AGM dinner of the IMA, May.

Schinasi, G., B. Drees and W. Lee (1999), 'Managing global finance and risk', *Finance and Development*, December.

UBS (2008), *Shareholder Report on UBS's Write-down*, Zurich: UBS, April.

ABOUT THE IEA

The Institute is a research and educational charity (No. CC 235 351), limited by guarantee. Its mission is to improve understanding of the fundamental institutions of a free society by analysing and expounding the role of markets in solving economic and social problems.

The IEA achieves its mission by:

- a high-quality publishing programme
- conferences, seminars, lectures and other events
- outreach to school and college students
- brokering media introductions and appearances

The IEA, which was established in 1955 by the late Sir Antony Fisher, is an educational charity, not a political organisation. It is independent of any political party or group and does not carry on activities intended to affect support for any political party or candidate in any election or referendum, or at any other time. It is financed by sales of publications, conference fees and voluntary donations.

In addition to its main series of publications the IEA also publishes a quarterly journal, *Economic Affairs*.

The IEA is aided in its work by a distinguished international Academic Advisory Council and an eminent panel of Honorary Fellows. Together with other academics, they review prospective IEA publications, their comments being passed on anonymously to authors. All IEA papers are therefore subject to the same rigorous independent refereeing process as used by leading academic journals.

IEA publications enjoy widespread classroom use and course adoptions in schools and universities. They are also sold throughout the world and often translated/reprinted.

Since 1974 the IEA has helped to create a worldwide network of 100 similar institutions in over 70 countries. They are all independent but share the IEA's mission.

Views expressed in the IEA's publications are those of the authors, not those of the Institute (which has no corporate view), its Managing Trustees, Academic Advisory Council members or senior staff.

Members of the Institute's Academic Advisory Council, Honorary Fellows, Trustees and Staff are listed on the following page.

The Institute gratefully acknowledges financial support for its publications programme and other work from a generous benefaction by the late Alec and Beryl Warren.

Other papers recently published by the IEA include:

A Market in Airport Slots
Keith Boyfield (editor), David Starkie, Tom Bass & Barry Humphreys
Readings 56; ISBN 0 255 36505 5; £10.00

Money, Inflation and the Constitutional Position of the Central Bank
Milton Friedman & Charles A. E. Goodhart
Readings 57; ISBN 0 255 36538 1; £10.00

railway.com
Parallels between the Early British Railways and the ICT Revolution
Robert C. B. Miller
Research Monograph 57; ISBN 0 255 36534 9; £12.50

The Regulation of Financial Markets
Edited by Philip Booth & David Currie
Readings 58; ISBN 0 255 36551 9; £12.50

Climate Alarmism Reconsidered
Robert L. Bradley Jr
Hobart Paper 146; ISBN 0 255 36541 1; £12.50

Government Failure: E. G. West on Education
Edited by James Tooley & James Stanfield
Occasional Paper 130; ISBN 0 255 36552 7; £12.50

Corporate Governance: Accountability in the Marketplace
Elaine Sternberg
Second edition
Hobart Paper 147; ISBN 0 255 36542 x; £12.50

The Land Use Planning System
Evaluating Options for Reform
John Corkindale
Hobart Paper 148; ISBN 0 255 36550 0; £10.00

Economy and Virtue
Essays on the Theme of Markets and Morality
Edited by Dennis O'Keeffe
Readings 59; ISBN 0 255 36504 7; £12.50

Free Markets Under Siege
Cartels, Politics and Social Welfare
Richard A. Epstein
Occasional Paper 132; ISBN 0 255 36553 5; £10.00

Unshackling Accountants
D. R. Myddelton
Hobart Paper 149; ISBN 0 255 36559 4; £12.50

The Euro as Politics
Pedro Schwartz
Research Monograph 58; ISBN 0 255 36535 7; £12.50

Pricing Our Roads
Vision and Reality
Stephen Glaister & Daniel J. Graham
Research Monograph 59; ISBN 0 255 36562 4; £10.00

The Role of Business in the Modern World
Progress, Pressures, and Prospects for the Market Economy
David Henderson
Hobart Paper 150; ISBN 0 255 36548 9; £12.50

Public Service Broadcasting Without the BBC?
Alan Peacock
Occasional Paper 133; ISBN 0 255 36565 9; £10.00

The ECB and the Euro: the First Five Years
Otmar Issing
Occasional Paper 134; ISBN 0 255 36555 1; £10.00

Towards a Liberal Utopia?
Edited by Philip Booth
Hobart Paperback 32; ISBN 0 255 36563 2; £15.00

The Way Out of the Pensions Quagmire
Philip Booth & Deborah Cooper
Research Monograph 60; ISBN 0 255 36517 9; £12.50

Black Wednesday
A Re-examination of Britain's Experience in the Exchange Rate Mechanism
Alan Budd
Occasional Paper 135; ISBN 0 255 36566 7; £7.50

Crime: Economic Incentives and Social Networks
Paul Ormerod
Hobart Paper 151; ISBN 0 255 36554 3; £10.00

The Road to Serfdom *with* **The Intellectuals and Socialism**
Friedrich A. Hayek
Occasional Paper 136; ISBN 0 255 36576 4; £10.00

Money and Asset Prices in Boom and Bust
Tim Congdon
Hobart Paper 152; ISBN 0 255 36570 5; £10.00

The Dangers of Bus Re-regulation
and Other Perspectives on Markets in Transport
John Hibbs et al.
Occasional Paper 137; ISBN 0 255 36572 1; £10.00

The New Rural Economy
Change, Dynamism and Government Policy
Berkeley Hill et al.
Occasional Paper 138; ISBN 0 255 36546 2; £15.00

The Benefits of Tax Competition
Richard Teather
Hobart Paper 153; ISBN 0 255 36569 1; £12.50

Wheels of Fortune
Self-funding Infrastructure and the Free Market Case for a Land Tax
Fred Harrison
Hobart Paper 154; ISBN 0 255 36589 6; £12.50

Were 364 Economists All Wrong?
Edited by Philip Booth
Readings 60; ISBN 978 0 255 36588 8; £10.00

Europe After the 'No' Votes
Mapping a New Economic Path
Patrick A. Messerlin
Occasional Paper 139; ISBN 978 0 255 36580 2; £10.00

The Railways, the Market and the Government
John Hibbs et al.
Readings 61; ISBN 978 0 255 36567 3; £12.50

Corruption: The World's Big C
Cases, Causes, Consequences, Cures
Ian Senior
Research Monograph 61; ISBN 978 0 255 36571 0; £12.50

Choice and the End of Social Housing
Peter King
Hobart Paper 155; ISBN 978 0 255 36568 0; £10.00

Sir Humphrey's Legacy
Facing Up to the Cost of Public Sector Pensions
Neil Record
Hobart Paper 156; ISBN 978 0 255 36578 9; £10.00

The Economics of Law
Cento Veljanovski
Second edition
Hobart Paper 157; ISBN 978 0 255 36561 1; £12.50

Living with Leviathan
Public Spending, Taxes and Economic Performance
David B. Smith
Hobart Paper 158; ISBN 978 0 255 36579 6; £12.50

The Vote Motive
Gordon Tullock
New edition
Hobart Paperback 33; ISBN 978 0 255 36577 2; £10.00

Waging the War of Ideas
John Blundell
Third edition
Occasional Paper 131; ISBN 978 0 255 36606 9; £12.50

The War Between the State and the Family
How Government Divides and Impoverishes
Patricia Morgan
Hobart Paper 159; ISBN 978 0 255 36596 3; £10.00

Capitalism – A Condensed Version
Arthur Seldon
Occasional Paper 140; ISBN 978 0 255 36598 7; £7.50

Catholic Social Teaching and the Market Economy
Edited by Philip Booth
Hobart Paperback 34; ISBN 978 0 255 36581 9; £15.00

Adam Smith – A Primer
Eamonn Butler
Occasional Paper 141; ISBN 978 0 255 36608 3; £7.50

Happiness, Economics and Public Policy
Helen Johns & Paul Ormerod
Research Monograph 62; ISBN 978 0 255 36600 7; £10.00

They Meant Well
Government Project Disasters
D. R. Myddelton
Hobart Paper 160; ISBN 978 0 255 36601 4; £12.50

Rescuing Social Capital from Social Democracy
John Meadowcroft & Mark Pennington
Hobart Paper 161; ISBN 978 0 255 36592 5; £10.00

Paths to Property
Approaches to Institutional Change in International Development
Karol Boudreaux & Paul Dragos Aligica
Hobart Paper 162; ISBN 978 0 255 36582 6; £10.00

Prohibitions
Edited by John Meadowcroft
Hobart Paperback 35; ISBN 978 0 255 36585 7; £15.00

Trade Policy, New Century
The WTO, FTAs and Asia Rising
Razeen Sally
Hobart Paper 163; ISBN 978 0 255 36544 4; £12.50

Sixty Years On – Who Cares for the NHS?
Helen Evans
Research Monograph 63; ISBN 978 0 255 36611 3; £10.00

Taming Leviathan
Waging the War of Ideas Around the World
Edited by Colleen Dyble
Occasional Paper 142; ISBN 978 0 255 36607 6; £12.50

The Legal Foundations of Free Markets
Edited by Stephen F. Copp
Hobart Paperback 36; ISBN 978 0 255 36591 8; £15.00

Climate Change Policy: Challenging the Activists
Edited by Colin Robinson
Readings 62; ISBN 978 0 255 36595 6; £10.00

Should We Mind the Gap?
Gender Pay Differentials and Public Policy
J. R. Shackleton
Hobart Paper 164; ISBN 978 0 255 36604 5; £10.00

Pension Provision: Government Failure Around the World
Edited by Philip Booth et al.
Readings 63; ISBN 978 0 255 36602 1; £15.00

New Europe's Old Regions
Piotr Zientara
Hobart Paper 165; ISBN 978 0 255 36617 5; £12.50

Central Banking in a Free Society
Tim Congdon
Hobart Paper 166; ISBN 978 0 255 36623 6; £12.50

Other IEA publications

Comprehensive information on other publications and the wider work of the IEA can be found at www.iea.org.uk. To order any publication please see below.

Personal customers

Orders from personal customers should be directed to the IEA:
Bob Layson
IEA
2 Lord North Street
FREEPOST LON10168
London SW1P 3YZ
Tel: 020 7799 8909. Fax: 020 7799 2137
Email: blayson@iea.org.uk

Trade customers

All orders from the book trade should be directed to the IEA's distributor:
Gazelle Book Services Ltd (IEA Orders)
FREEPOST RLYS-EAHU-YSCZ
White Cross Mills
Hightown
Lancaster LA1 4XS
Tel: 01524 68765, Fax: 01524 53232
Email: sales@gazellebooks.co.uk

IEA subscriptions

The IEA also offers a subscription service to its publications. For a single annual payment (currently £42.00 in the UK), subscribers receive every monograph the IEA publishes. For more information please contact:
Adam Myers
Subscriptions
IEA
2 Lord North Street
FREEPOST LON10168
London SW1P 3YZ
Tel: 020 7799 8920, Fax: 020 7799 2137
Email: amyers@iea.org.uk